The Forgotten Commandment

A Practical Guide to Loving Your Neighbour

by

Lauren Gush

The Forgotten Commandment

A Practical Guide to Loving Your Neighbour

ISBN 978-0-7961-0039-9

lauren@gushfamily.net

Cover Design: Robert E. Blignaut

Printed in South Africa

Contents

Acknowledgements

Thank you to everyone who has been part of this journey. This book was conceived and written during a very difficult time in my life, and I would not have got through it without each and every one of you. I will always be grateful for your love, support, encouragement, and belief in me.

First and foremost, I give all the honour and glory to my Lord Jesus Christ. He gave me the title of this book during a time when I was feeling lost and questioning my purpose, and He made a way forward for me. Every single word on these pages is His and I am so grateful that He chose to use me to bring His message of love to people.

To my husband Andrew and my incredible daughters Kate and Alison, I have no words to express my love and gratitude. You have been unfailing in your encouragement, understanding and support of me and I couldn't wish for a better team of cheerleaders! I love you!

To my amazing parents, Brian and Janice, I would not be who I am today without you. Thank you for setting such a wonderful example of godly marriage and a life of faithful commitment to the Lord. Thank you for always wanting the best for me and for your unconditional love.

To Rob, my sounding board, truth-teller, cover designer and motivator when I needed it, thank you and I love you.

To Bets, thank you for giving up your valuable time to proof-read my book and for your never-ending encouragement and support. Your friendship and your wisdom are blessings from Heaven!

To Lee, Carolyn, Daphne, Carol and Gert, your enthusiasm, excitement, and encouragement have been invaluable to me. I consider myself so lucky to have friends like you by my side.

Introduction

THIS IS NOT JUST ANOTHER BOOK ABOUT LOVE. THIS IS A BOOK about understanding God's heart and allowing it to change the way that you love. All of us, no matter what our position, job, or title, have many opportunities to impact people.

Stop and think for a minute about all the people that you come into contact with on a daily basis. Your husband or wife, your children, your siblings, your parents. And that's just in your home! What about friends, work colleagues, employees, the stranger on the street, and the homeless man on the corner.

Be honest with yourself for a moment. Do you love every single one of those people? I'm not talking about emotional love or conditional human love; I am talking about the kind of love that Jesus commands us to have for one another. I'm talking about "agape" love. And yes, it was a commandment! If I am totally honest with myself, I would probably have to say "No", and I am sure you would too.

I *do* know that Jesus would not have told us to do something that is not within our ability (aided by the power of the Holy Spirit) to do. So, if you, like me, truly want to understand what it means and what it looks like to love your neighbour, then this book is for you.

I have called this book "The Forgotten Commandment". Let me explain a bit further.

In Matthew 22, Jesus is being questioned by a group of Pharisees. He had just silenced some of the Sadducees with His teachings and, hearing this, the Pharisees sought to test Him. One of them, a lawyer by profession, asks Jesus a loaded question – one he hopes will catch the Messiah out. In verse 36, he asks: "Teacher, which is the great commandment in the law?"

Bear in mind that these are very well educated, learned men who have devoted themselves to the study of the Scriptures. If there was a Scripture, they knew it. In their minds, following the Old Testament law was the only path to righteousness. Their hope was that Jesus would deviate from the Scriptures and, in so doing, give them something to hold against Him.

In Matthew 22 v 37 - 39, we read Jesus' reply to the Pharisee:

Jesus said to him, "'You shall love the Lord your God with all your heart, with all your soul, and with all your mind.' This is the first and great commandment. And the second is like it: 'You shall love your neighbour as yourself.'"

This answer would have been familiar to the Pharisees. Jesus was quoting directly from the Old Testament Scriptures found in Deuteronomy 6 v 5 and Leviticus 19 v 18.

The Old Testament Law and the New Testament Gospel of Grace both teach the same thing - how to love God and how to love one another.

Simple, isn't it? And yet, the religious leaders of Jesus' time became so obsessed with the "detail" and the "doing" that they lost sight of the main objective. They did not love God with all their hearts, minds and souls and they also did not love their neighbours.

The sad fact is that if you are a Christian in today's world trying to love people the way we are called to, you are probably met with a fair amount of judgement, ridicule, and suspicion. You might be told you feel too deeply, that your expectations of friends are too high, or that you invest too much in people. After many years of experiencing exactly these reactions, and seeking the Lord about it, I have only one response. How invested was Jesus when He went to the Cross for you? How deeply did He feel for you when He overcame His own flesh in the Garden of Gethsemane? He was and still is the ultimate model of love that we have been called to imitate.

Christians today know the Scripture that Jesus quoted in Matthew 22 pretty well. In fact, most of us can probably quote it by heart. The commandment to love God with all our heart, soul and mind is something that makes sense to us. After all, He is God and He is worthy of all our love and all our focus. It's the commandment to love our neighbour as ourselves that leaves us shifting uncomfortably in our seats. It's too difficult. It's not possible. Let's forget that part.

The Forgotten Commandment.

CHAPTER
One

God's Love for You

God loves each one of us as if there were only one of us. – St. Augustine of Hippo

U NITED STATES AIRFORCE COLONEL JOHN MANSUR TELLS the story of an eight-year-old Vietnamese girl who was wounded in a misdirected mortar attack that struck an orphanage during the Vietnam War. A United States Navy doctor and nurse were called, and they quickly determined that the little girl would die if she did not receive a blood transfusion. Blood tests showed that none of the medical personnel had a compatible blood type, but several of the uninjured orphans did.

The doctor spoke a few words of broken Vietnamese, and the nurse a little bit of high-school French. Using that combination, together with sign language, they tried to explain to their young, frightened audience that unless they could replace some of the girl's lost blood, she would certainly die. They then asked if anyone would be willing to donate blood to help the little girl.

Their request was met with wide-eyed silence. After several long moments, a small boy raised his hand slowly and waveringly, dropped it back down, and then put it up again.

"Oh, thank you," said the nurse in French. "What is your name?"

"Heng," came the reply.

Heng was quickly laid on a pallet, his arm swabbed with alcohol, and a needle inserted into his vein. Throughout this ordeal Heng lay stiff and silent. After a moment, he let out a shuddering sob and covered his small face with his free hand. His sobs gave way to steady, silent crying.

The medical team was concerned. Something was obviously very wrong. At this point, a Vietnamese nurse arrived to help. Seeing Heng's distress, she spoke to him rapidly in Vietnamese, listened to his reply and answered him in a soothing voice. After a moment, the boy stopped crying and a look of great relief spread over his face. Glancing up, the nurse said quietly to the Americans, "He thought he was dying. He misunderstood you. He thought you had asked him to give all of his blood so the little girl could live."

"But why would he be willing to do that?" asked the Navy nurse.

The Vietnamese nurse repeated the question to the little boy, who answered simply, "She's my friend."

What I love about this story is that it highlights the personal nature of sacrificial love. It's quite easy for us to understand how someone could sacrifice their life in a grand heroic gesture to save hundreds or thousands of other people, but how many would do it to save just one?

I know someone who did!

There are many Scriptures in the Bible that tell us very clearly that God loves us. Most people, even non-Christians, can quote John 3 v 16, which says:

For God so loved the world that He gave His only begotten Son, that whoever believes in Him should not perish but have everlasting life.

This verse tells us that God sent Jesus because He loved the "world", which encompasses all of mankind. This is absolutely true. However, God's love and grace towards you is not just part of a package deal because you are one of millions of people who has chosen to believe in Him. His love for you is intensely personal. He loved you before you were even born (Jeremiah 1 v 5), and He created you specifically for His glory and His pleasure (Revelation 4 v 11). He desired relationship with you so much that He sent the Holy Spirit to you at exactly the right time and in exactly the right way to offer you the gift of eternal life.

Matthew 10 v 29 – 31 shows us just how intimately He knows and values us:

Are not two sparrows sold for a copper coin? And not one of them falls to the ground apart from your Father's will. But the very hairs of your head are all numbered. Do not fear therefore; you are of more value than many sparrows.

Think for a minute of your most intimate and personal relationship. You might know a lot about that person, but you certainly don't know how many hairs are on their head! We don't even know the number of hairs on our own heads! This illustrates that there is no detail about us, however insignificant, that God does not know. He relates to you as an individual, as a Father to a child. Jesus did die for all mankind, but He also went to the cross for you personally.

C.S. Lewis echoes this truth in the following quote:

"When Christ died, He died for you individually just as much as if you'd been the only man in the world."

If you struggle to believe that Jesus loved you enough to die for you alone, don't be disheartened. You are not the only one! Many Christians face this battle on a daily basis. All of us have grown up in a society that is so performance-based that we have difficulty accepting that Jesus would make such a sacrifice for us even though we mess up and make mistakes on a daily basis. Paul acknowledges this in the following Scripture:

For when we were still without strength, in due time Christ died for the ungodly. For scarcely for a righteous man will one die; yet perhaps for a good man someone would even dare to die. But God demonstrates His own love toward us, in that while we were still sinners, Christ died for us.

Romans 5 v 6 – 8

There are many Bible verses that speak of the free gifts of salvation, righteousness, and eternal life through Jesus Christ. And they are just that, gifts given freely and unconditionally to each one of us, motivated by His overwhelming love for us. The key to understanding the nature of God's love for you is in realising that there is nothing you can do to make Him love you more than He already does. Conversely, there is nothing you can do to make Him love you any less either! He already knew every sin you would commit and every wrong thought you would ever have before He sent Jesus to the Cross for you!

As I am typing these words, I am aware that I know all of this intellectually, but the question is: Do I have revelation of it as spiritual truth? Am I so settled in the knowledge of His love that I will never question it again? Revelation is a term that is used a lot in churches and religious circles, but I am not convinced that everyone understands what it really means.

In 1 John 4 v 16 it says:

And we have known and believed the love that God has for us. God is love, and he who abides in love abides in God, and God in him.

Notice that in this verse it speaks of "knowing" and "believing". They are two completely different things. "Knowing" happens in our brains when we receive and store information. If we "know" something it means we acknowledge it as fact for some or other reason. Many times, it is because we received the information from a source we see as an authority, such as a textbook or a teacher for instance. Other times, we can acquire knowledge through experience. It is defined in the Oxford Dictionary as "facts, information, and skills acquired through experience or education."

"Believing" happens in the heart. It is an acceptance that something exists and is true, especially when there is no proof. Once we believe something in our hearts, we then start to see the impact of it in our lives.

Head knowledge remains just that. Heart knowledge has an outworking and a tangible impact. In the context of God's love, we can "know" He loves us because the Bible tells us He does. We have no physical proof of God's love, especially if we have not experienced it for ourselves. So how do we make the leap from knowing to believing? The answer is revelation. Revelation bridges the gap between knowledge and belief.

We need to realise that revelation happens in the spirit; it is not something we can achieve in our own ability through effort or study. Yes, it is important that we spend time studying the Bible and meditating on God's word, but we have to do it in partnership with the Holy Spirit. Revelation comes when the Holy Spirit takes a truth and makes it come alive on the inside of us. When this happens, it is irreversible!

I have a close friend who, during his personal time with the Lord, received an instantaneous revelation of God's love for him. The Lord showed him in a vision how He held him in His hands like a precious pearl and allowed him a brief glimpse of His feelings towards him. This experience had a profound effect on my friend and changed his relationship with the Lord forever. Since that moment, no matter what he has faced, he has never doubted God's love for him. It truly is settled in his heart. This is what we all need!

I don't think that any of us will fully understand the extent of God's love for us until we stand in His Presence one day, but it is something that we need to seek and ask the Holy Spirit to reveal to us. Paul understood the importance of this and in his letter to the Ephesians, he prayed the following prayer:

That Christ may dwell in your hearts through faith; that you, being rooted and grounded in love, may be able to comprehend with all the saints what is the width and length and depth and height— to know the love of Christ which passes knowledge; that you may be filled with all the fullness of God.

Ephesians 3 v 17 - 19

In this Scripture, Paul clearly states that in order to experience the fullness of God we need to "know the love of Christ which passes knowledge". He is speaking about revelation knowledge, which is spiritual truth becoming reality. When the reality of God's love for us starts to take root in our hearts, we can begin to take hold of everything He has made available to us as His children. Underpinned by the foundation of His love, we can live abundant and impactful lives, free of condemnation and the need to perform. Sounds good, doesn't it?

Understanding God's love is not only essential for us as individuals, but also for those around us. There is a legal term called the Nemo Dat Rule. The name comes from the Latin phrase "Nemo dat quod non habet" which, directly translated, means "no one can give away that which they do not have". While this is true in the physical realm, it is also an important spiritual principle. If we have not received and experienced the love of God, we will not be able to show His love to others.

I like to use the analogy of fire to explain this concept. An unlit candle cannot light another candle. We have to make sure that we spend time close to Jesus, so that we catch alight with His fire. Only then can we pass that flame on to the people around us. The revelation of God's love for us sets us alight and allows us to minister to others straight from the source of love that is never depleted. So many people, especially those in ministry, end up exhausted and burnt out from trying to love others in their own strength. God's love for us is a wellspring that never runs dry. Once we understand how much He loves us, we can allow His love to overflow from within us to impact every person we meet.

If you need a deeper understanding of God's love for you, here are some pointers on where to start:

1.   Pray

But the Helper, the Holy Spirit, whom the Father will send in My name, He will teach you all things, and bring to your remembrance all things that I said to you.

John 14 v 26

We have access to the One who teaches us all things! We only have to ask. I have never failed to be amazed by how quick He is to demonstrate His love for me when I ask Him to do so! Give it a try!

2.   Meditate on the Word

It is vital that we spend time reading Scripture when we are trusting the Holy Spirit to give us revelation of God's love for us. He will most often use God's Word to teach us, although it is not the only way. Meditate on Scriptures that speak of God's character and His goodness towards us. Allow the Holy Spirit to make the Word come alive in your heart.

3.   Pray in tongues

But you, beloved, building yourselves up on your most holy faith, praying in the Holy Spirit, keep yourselves in the love of God, looking for the mercy of our Lord Jesus Christ unto eternal life.

Jude 20 - 21

According to this Scripture, praying in the Holy Spirit keeps us in the love of God, which is right where we need to be. When we pray in tongues, our born-again spirit is communicating directly with God. We can be confident that these prayers are powerful and accurate, and directly in line with God's will for us. The Bible tells us that praying in the Spirit edifies us and promotes spiritual growth.

Wherever you are in your journey with Christ, I hope that you have come to the end of this chapter feeling encouraged and excited to discover more about God's love for you. A true understanding of His heart for you will change not only your life, but also the lives of those around you.

If you need more information on what it means to be born again, or on speaking in tongues, please refer to the back of this book.

CHAPTER
Two

Forms of Love

There are as many forms of love as there are moments in time. - Jane Austen

T HE MESSAGE IN THIS BOOK HAS BEEN IN MY HEART FOR A very long time. I have always been a "lover" by nature, even before I was born again and got to know Jesus. From a young age, I found myself drawn to the lonely, hurting, and broken people who crossed my path. As far back as I can remember, I always believed that love could overcome any obstacle.

When I was in my late twenties, I met someone who became one of the closest friends I have ever had. For the purposes of the story, let's call her Jane. I met Jane at ante-natal classes at our local hospital when we were both pregnant with our first children who were born just a few weeks apart. It was one of those friendships where you feel an immediate connection and it's like you have known each other for years. We started to spend a lot of time together after our babies were born and quickly became the best of friends. Jane, I learned, had struggled with drug addiction in her past but had been clean for several years when we met. Sadly, her struggle with addiction continued and, over the next few years, she relapsed on numerous occasions. Each relapse and subsequent period in rehabilitation facilities was devastating. My response was to try and love her out of her addiction. After all, love is more powerful than addiction, isn't it? Over the next few years, I became not just a best friend, but a chaperone, a minder and a policewoman all rolled into one.

Inevitably, after one of her relapses, I reached the point of breakdown. I just could not carry on anymore and I had to remove myself, and my family, from the situation. I remember that night crying and saying to my husband that everything I had believed was a lie – that love made no difference. I was right, but I was also wrong. The point that I was missing was that I was trying to change Jane with my own flawed and powerless human love when what she really needed was the love of her Saviour. What I had believed since childhood, that love could overcome even the most difficult obstacles, was true. Love *is* enough. But this is only true of God's kind of love.

Let's be clear, without understanding the true nature of love, we will never be able to love people in the way Jesus commanded us to love. The journey to understanding God's kind of love is one we cannot afford not to take. The Scriptures make this abundantly clear.

In 1 Corinthians 13 v 1 - 3 it says:

Though I speak with the tongues of men and of angels, but have not love, I have become sounding brass or a clanging cymbal. And though I have the gift of prophecy, and understand all mysteries and all knowledge, and though I have all faith, so that I could remove mountains, but have not love, I am nothing. And though I bestow all my goods to feed the poor, and though I give my body to be burned, but have not love, it profits me nothing.

That's quite an eye-opening Scripture, isn't it? It certainly made me stop and think. You could be the most gifted preacher or teacher, a respected, God-ordained prophet, a learned, wise intellectual or a paragon of faith, but if you do not have love, then you have nothing. This Scripture does not say you might lack something – it says you have *nothing.* Those important and sought-after positions, giftings and callings that many of us want are worthless if we do not have love. If there is one thing that we should take away from this Scripture, it is that our emphasis should not be so much on what we do, but rather on how we do it.

This point is underscored by what Paul says in 1 Corinthians 13 v 3. We could give away all our worldly possessions to the poor and still not have love. How can this be? Is this not the very description of charity? "Charity" is an old English word that was used to describe love that results in action. Isn't that the definition of God's kind of love?

What is important here is not the action, but the heart behind it. It is relatively easy to give away money and worldly possessions (especially if you are wealthy) to be seen as giving and generous. The motivation behind the giving, however, is not love, but rather glory and affirmation for oneself. Giving that is motivated by God's kind of love should be done in secret, as the Scripture instructs in Matthew 6 v 3:

But when you do a charitable deed, do not let your left hand know what your right hand is doing.

The driving force behind our actions *must* be God's kind of love otherwise our actions are worth nothing.

At the time that the books of the New Testament were written, there were multiple words in the ancient Greek language that were used to describe love. The four words most commonly used were "Storge", "Eros", "Philia" and "Agape".

"Storge" could be described as affection or familial love. It is the natural or instinctual love that family members have for one another simply because they are related. An example of this would be the love of a parent for a child, or the love between siblings.

"Eros" was used to describe physical love or sexual desire. It is the type of love that involves lust, passion and romance and specifically relates to fulfilling an appetite. This is the type of love that should only be found in the context of marriage between a husband and a wife. "Eros" also denotes a love that is consuming and causes people to become preoccupied with each other.

"Philia" is the Greek word for affectionate love and describes the type of love you would find between good friends who are brought together by mutual interests. Interestingly, "philia" is the opposite of "phobia". The result of phobia is fleeing or separation, while the result of philia is a drawing together. As C.S. Lewis wrote in his book , The Four Loves:

"To the Ancients, Friendship seemed the happiest and most fully human of all loves."

Most of us reading this book will know and have experienced these three types of love described above, but it's the fourth type that we are interested in on this journey we are undertaking.

"Agape" speaks of a love that is sacrificial and unconditional by nature. Agape love is not concerned with self, but rather concerned with the greater good of another person. It is not motivated by feelings, attraction, or emotions, but is a conscious choice to love based on values and beliefs. To put this in context - when we love people with God's kind of love, we do not love them because they are lovely. We love them because God has commanded us to do so. We love people because we love God (the first commandment), and people are made in His image. This is God's kind of love – it consistently seeks and values the good of someone else above ourselves.

In the English language we have just one word to describe so many types of love. It's no wonder the word "love" has lost its meaning. We love our spouses and our children, we love friends, we love animals, we love certain types of food, we love travelling or playing sport. It's the same word, but not the same heart behind it, one would hope! I would certainly sacrifice for my children and put their needs ahead of mine, but I would not make the same sacrifice for my favourite food!

Most people today would consider love to be just another feeling or emotion like happiness, fear, guilt, or anger. There are two things to note about emotions. Firstly, they are temporary and secondly, they are conditional. Emotions are a response to our environment and our circumstances. I might feel happy today because someone paid me a nice compliment or gave me a gift. In other words, my circumstances dictate my emotions. Tomorrow, however, I might wake up not feeling happy anymore which demonstrates that emotions are temporary. Sadly, society has applied the same principles to love. I feel in love with my husband today, perhaps because he spent time with me and took me to dinner. Then he goes through a busy patch at work and cannot spend time with me and suddenly I don't feel in love anymore. Do you see what I am trying to illustrate? Emotions are conditional, and they are temporary.

So, we now know enough to be able to differentiate between agape love or God's kind of love, and other types of human love. God's kind of love is not an emotion. It is not temporary and is not affected by circumstances. On the contrary, agape love is two things. Firstly, it is a choice to seek the good of someone else regardless of feelings, behaviour, and circumstances. And, secondly, it is a love that results in action.

Understanding that God's kind of love is different to the love we find in the world was the first step in this journey we are taking. Now we need to find out what this love looks like. As in every situation, the answer can be found in the Word. In this case, both the written Word and the Living Word.

Let's read the biblical definition of love as we find it in 1 Corinthians 13 and then in the next chapter we will explore in more detail what it actually means.

1 Corinthians 13 v 4 – 8 reads as follows:

Love suffers long and is kind; love does not envy; love does not parade itself, is not puffed up; does not behave rudely, does not seek its own, is not provoked, thinks no evil; does not rejoice in iniquity, but rejoices in the truth; bears all things, believes all things, hopes all things, endures all things. Love never fails.

Let's look at another translation. The Message Bible puts it this way:

Love never gives up.
Love cares more for others than for self.
Love doesn't want what it doesn't have.
Love doesn't strut,
Doesn't have a swelled head,
Doesn't force itself on others,
Isn't always "me first",
Doesn't fly off the handle,
Doesn't keep score of the sins of others,
Doesn't revel when others grovel,
Takes pleasure in the flowering of truth,
Puts up with anything,
Trusts God always,
Always looks for the best,
Never looks back,
But keeps going to the end.
Love never dies.

If, like me, you are questioning if it is even possible for us as humans to love like this, just bear with me! This journey we are undertaking is not about condemnation or about making anyone feel like they are falling short. This is about understanding the commandment to love one another and discovering that, with the help of the Holy Spirit, we can do it!

CHAPTER
Three

God's Kind of Love

God's love is like an ocean. You can see its beginning, but not its end. – Rick Warren

T O RECAP, WE LEARNED IN THE PREVIOUS CHAPTER ABOUT God's kind of love, or agape love. It is a love that always seeks the best for others, regardless of self. It is sacrificial by nature and demands action. This is the way we have been called to love one another according to the Scriptures.

The Bible tells us very clearly that God *is* love. This means that not only is He the source of agape love, but that it is His very nature. Think about it – the greatest act of sacrificial love was God sending His only Son to die on the Cross for us. What an incomprehensible sacrifice He made on our behalf!

But God demonstrates His own love towards us, in that while we were still sinners, Christ died for us.

Romans 5 v 8

The Scripture in Romans 5 v 8 perfectly describes agape love - action that was sacrificial and unconditional in nature. Jesus needs to be our blueprint and our source. We cannot operate in agape love towards others if we are not personally experiencing it in relationship with God. The following Scriptures confirm this:

He who does not love does not know God, for God is love.

1 John 4 v 8

And we have known and believed the love that God has for us. God is love, and he who abides in love abides in God, and God in him.

1 John 4 v 16

In this chapter, let's dive a little deeper into the meaning of agape love as described by Paul in 1 Corinthians 13. If we are serious about operating in God's kind of love, we need to have a good understanding of what it looks like.

As a reminder, 1 Corinthians 13 v 4 – 8 reads as follows:

Love suffers long and is kind; love does not envy; love does not parade itself, is not puffed up; does not behave rudely, does not seek its own, is not provoked, thinks no evil; does not rejoice in iniquity, but rejoices in the truth; bears all things, believes all things, hopes all things, endures all things. Love never fails.

Let's examine each of these characteristics one at a time, using Strong's Concordance to help us to understand the meaning of the ancient Greek root words.

1. Love suffers long.

   Longsuffering = Makrothymeō [Strong's G3115]

   The Greek word for long-suffering is "makrothymeō", made up of the words "makros" (long) and "thumia" (temper, passion, emotion). This literally means to be long-tempered as opposed to short-tempered. It speaks of patience, self-control, restraint, or tolerance in the face of provocation or unfavourable circumstances. It is the capacity to be wronged and not retaliate.

   The Bible uses this word many times to illustrate God's patience towards sinful mankind but is also used in Scripture as one of the fruits of the Holy Spirit (Galatians 5 v 22 - 23) and one of the characteristics of the love we are commanded to demonstrate towards our neighbours.

   George writes that makrothymeō:

   "... is the ability to put up with other people even when that is not an easy thing to do. Patience in this sense, of course, is preeminently a characteristic of God, who is "long-suffering" with his rebellious creatures. He is the loving Lord who in the face of obstinate infidelity and repeated rejection still says of his people, "How can I give you up, Ephraim? How can I hand you over, Israel?" (Hosea 11:8). Paul's point is clear: if God has been so long-suffering with us, should we not display this same grace in our relationships with one another? This

31

quality should characterize the life of every believer, but it has a special relevance for those who are called to teach and preach the Word of God. As Paul instructed Timothy, "Preach (aorist imperative) the Word; be prepared in season and out of season; correct, rebuke and encourage— with great patience and careful instruction" (2 Timothy 4:2)." (George, T. The New American Commentary. Page 402. Nashville: Broadman & Holman Publishers.)

2. Love is kind.

    Kind = Chrēsteuomai [Strong's G5541]

The word "kind" found in this Scripture was translated from the Greek word "chrēsteuomai". This is the one and only time this word is found in the New Testament. It speaks of an attitude of being willing to help or assist in rendering service to others. In other words, "chrēsteuomai" is goodwill in action. This word suggests someone who is gentle, who can calm an upset person and help quietly in practical ways.

In the second century AD, the pagans referred to Christians as "chrēstinai" which literally translated means "those made up of kindness". This is how non-believers in that day experienced followers of Jesus Christ. I wonder if they would use the same name for Christians today.

I found this amazing example of kindness within marriage in a sermon entitled "Why Love Has a Bad Memory" by Dr. Ray Pritchard.

"In one of his news reports, Paul Harvey told about a man named Carl Coleman who was driving to work when a woman motorist, passing too close, snagged his fender with hers. Both cars stopped. The young woman surveying the damage was in tears. It was her fault, she admitted. But it was a new car...less than two days from the showroom. How was she ever going to face her husband? Mr. Coleman was sympathetic but explained they must note each other's license number and automobile registration. The woman reached into the glove compartment of her car to retrieve the documents in an envelope. And on the first paper to tumble out, in a heavy masculine scrawl, were these words: 'In case of accident, remember, Honey, it's you I love, not the car.'"

3. Love does not envy.

    Envy = Zēloō [Strong's G2206]

Now we start to explore some of the characteristics that love is *not*. The first of these in 1 Corinthians 13 is envy or jealousy. The root of this word in ancient Greek is "zēloō", from "zeo", which literally means "boil". If you have ever experienced jealousy, or the destructive impact of it, I'm sure you will agree that this makes complete sense. Interestingly, it can be used in a positive way when translated as "zeal".

In the context of describing what love is not, "zēloō" here is translated as the negative emotion of jealousy. This jealousy can take two different forms. The first is when a person sets their heart on something belonging to someone else. We may also recognise this as coveting or covetousness. The second is when one experiences negative feelings regarding the success, status, or achievements of another person.

These two types of envy or jealousy have no place in agape love. Love is totally satisfied with what it has and rejoices for someone else because of what they have. Secondly, love never begrudges the success or achievement of another person, but rather delights in it for their sake.

Augustine wrote: "The reason why love does not envy is because it is not puffed up. For where puffing up precedes, envy follows, because pride is the mother of envy."

Jealousy was one of the sins causing hurt in the church at Corinth. The people had divided into factions because they were jealous of one another's gifts. In 1 Corinthians 12 v 31, Paul instructs them to follow the "more excellent way" of love, before going on to tell them in 1 Corinthians 13 v 4 that "love does not envy".

4. Love does not parade itself; is not puffed up.
    Boastful = Perpereuomai [Strong's G4068]
    Arrogant/Proud = Physioō [Strong's G5448]

These characteristics of speak of pride. Agape love is not proud or boastful since its nature is to focus on others first. True agape love never has to try and prove itself by blowing its own trumpet or showing off in front of others. This is a love that works behind the scenes and is happy to do so. It does not need recognition or affirmation. The phrase "puffed up" literally means to have an exaggerated view of one's own importance.

Barclay writes that: "There is a self-effacing quality in love. True love will always be far more impressed with its own unworthiness than its own merit." (Barclay, W: The Daily Study Bible Series. The Westminster Press or Logos)

If love is primarily concerned with the welfare and well-being of others, there is no place for any focus on one's own status or position.

5. Love does not behave rudely.
    Act unbecomingly = Aschēmoneō [Strong's G807]

The Ancient Greek, translated in most Bibles as "behave rudely", actually means to behave in an ugly, indecent, or unbecoming manner. It speaks of someone who acts in a way that goes against social and moral standards. This type of behaviour more often than not results in embarrassment for other people. We tend to think that rudeness is limited to how we speak, but in this context, it also applies to manners, how one behaves and how one dresses. Someone who acts in an unbecoming manner shows a complete disregard for how his words or actions might affect other people.

The Forgotten Commandment

There seems to be a trend in the church environment at the moment whereby people feel it is acceptable to say anything to each other under the banner of telling the truth "in love". While there is biblical application and an appropriate time for this, it is not a license to deal carelessly with the feelings and sensitivities of others. It is not right to excuse someone who does this by saying "He means well," or "His heart is good." Simply put: If the end goal is love, then the means of getting there should be loving.

If we were looking for a way to describe how love would act that is not rude or unbecoming, we could say that love is tactful and careful with the feelings of other people.

6. Love does not seek its own.

> To seek = zēteō [Strong's G2212]
>
> Of himself = heautou [Strong's G1438]

This phrase, literally translated, means "does not seek the things of itself". Being self-seeking is the literally the opposite of love. Stop for a minute and think of all the words in the English language that start with "self". There are many!

To mention a few:

Self-assurance   Self-defence

Self-esteem   Self-image

Self-justification	Self-love
Self-confidence	Self-made
Self-obsessed	Self-motivated

We all fall into the trap of being self-focused every single day. This is the very nature of the flesh that we are called upon to resist and deny.

Jesus tells us in Luke 9 v 23:

If anyone wishes to come after Me, he must deny himself, and take up his cross and follow Me.

The antidote to this "self-focus" is to change our minds to be "God-focused". As soon as we do this, His kind of love can begin to transform us to become more focused on the needs of others than on our own needs.

MacArthur puts it very simply when he says: "Love that takes a person outside of himself and centers his attention on the well–being of others is the only cure for self–centeredness." (MacArthur, J: 1 Corinthians. Chicago: Moody Press or Logos)

7.   Love is not provoked.

Provoke = Paroxynō [Strong's G3947]

This Greek verb gives us our English word "paroxysm" which is defined as a fit, attack, a convulsion (like paroxysm of coughing) or a sudden violent outburst.

In the Bible, the word "paroxynō" means to upset someone and to cause anger in them. This word was used many times in the Old Testament, primarily to describe God's reaction to Israel when they sinned against Him.

In this verse, however, Paul is referring to a sinful type of anger, not the righteous anger of God. A person who is walking in agape love should never be provoked to this point, that is to the point of violent emotional outburst. When we walk in love, we are imitators of Christ and should be able to endure insults and provocation as He did. We find the perfect example of what to do when provoked in 1 Peter 2 v 21 - 23:

For to this you were called, because Christ also suffered
for us, leaving us an example, that you should follow His steps:

"Who committed no sin,
Nor was deceit found in His mouth";

who, when He was reviled, did not revile in return; when He suffered, He
did not threaten, but committed Himself to Him who judges righteously;

8. Love thinks no evil.

   Keeps record = Logizomai [Strong's G3049]

According to the original Greek text, these words can also be translated as "Love does not keep record of wrongs or past mistakes."

The Greek word for "keep record" was the word "logizomai" from "logos" which means "reason", "word" or "account". It was a word most often associated with the practice of book-keeping and was also used in the Scriptures where Paul speaks about sin being credited to man's account.

We can't really speak about keeping record of wrongs without touching on the issue of offense. Offense is a very powerful and often very destructive force. If someone has wronged you, it is appropriate for you to confront that person in love, and then to move on. If you cannot move on and your mind is held hostage by the offense, it means that you are keeping record of wrongs and are not operating in love. We should not be imputing people's wrongs to their account. In the same way that Jesus wiped our sins out of existence when He died on the Cross for us, we need to embody agape love by forgiving those who have wronged us.

I'm sure you will agree that this is one of those things that is easy to say, but not so easy to do. Thank you, Jesus, for giving us the Holy Spirit, because without Him we would never be able to walk in forgiveness!

If God's love and forgiveness for us was based on our love and forgiveness for others, we would all be in trouble!

9. Love does not rejoice in iniquity but rejoices in the Truth.
   Rejoice = Chairō [Strong's G5463]
   Iniquity = Adikia [Strong's G93]
   Truth = Alētheia [Strong's G225]

Using the ancient Greek words and their corresponding meanings, we could translate the above characteristic of love as follows: "Love is not happy or delighted where there is injustice or unrighteousness but rejoices in that which is not hidden."

"Truth" in this context can be described as "that which is not hidden" or "a declaration which has a corresponding reality". A lie or untruth hides what is true and words, whether spoken or written, are only true when they correspond with reality.

When we look at this particular characteristic of love, the context of "truth" goes way beyond the spoken or written word.

The word Paul uses points to a much broader concept of truth. It speaks of a moral truth that is based on the character of God Himself.

We can't talk about moral truth without talking about discrimination. It's a touchy subject in today's society because people have come to believe that love and acceptance are basically the same thing. If you love me, you must accept me and my behaviour. But let me throw a spanner in the works; Love *does* discriminate.

That statement may shock you, but it's true. Love chooses what and what not to rejoice in. This sounds crazy, especially in terms of todays culture, but agape love sometimes requires us to take a difficult stand.

In John 17 v 17, Jesus defines God's Word as truth. The Gospel is truth. The truth of what the Father did for us by sending Jesus to die for us is the most important truth that we could ever share with another person. Sharing truth with someone else can be tricky because truth by nature is exclusive. In other words, if I tell the truth, then by default anything else is a lie and people do not like to have their beliefs questioned. In a society where it is considered unloving to say that something or somebody is wrong, we need to learn from Jesus how to tell the truth in a way that is patient and kind, not arrogant or rude.

When people try to say that love demands acceptance of any belief or behaviour, we only have to go back and read 1 Corinthians 13 v 6. This Scripture doesn't simply tell us that if we love with God's kind of love then we must tell the truth. It tells us that agape love rejoices in the truth! We, as followers of Christ, should not apologise for or defend the truth in God's Word, but rather we should joyfully proclaim it.

We must deal kindly with one another when telling each other the truth. You can indeed have truth without love, but you cannot have love without truth. Ephesians 4 v 15 talks about "speaking the truth in love" which implies by contrast that you can speak the truth without love. Truth without love becomes a weapon – harming, alienating, and condemning people.

10. Love bears, believes, hopes, and endures all things.

   Bears = Stegō [Strong's G4722]

   Believes = Pisteuō [Strong's G4100]

   Hopes = Elpizō [Strong's G1679]

   Endures = Hypomenō [Strong's G5278]

The word "stegō", translated here as "bear" was used to describe how a roof protects a building, for example by keeping water out. Love bears all things by protecting others. This could be protection from actual physical harm or from emotional harm in the form of slander or gossip. God's kind of love does not gossip about others or listen to gossip. When someone is in the wrong, agape love does not protect the sin, but it does protect the sinner.

"Pisteuō" means to consider something as true. In the context of describing agape love, this means to have a firm belief in the goodness or ability of someone. It also speaks of putting one's trust in people. We should always give people the benefit of the doubt and give them the opportunity to prove themselves trustworthy. God's kind of love is not suspicious or distrustful.

The word for "hope" in this verse is the Greek word "elpizō" which means absolute assurance. It speaks of waiting with joy and confidence. Love is positive and has confidence in the future. Agape love seeks always to hope in God, in spite of circumstances. Even when met with disappointment, love still makes a conscious decision to expect the best and persevere. Agape love is optimistic!

"Hypomenō" means to abide, to persevere under misfortunes and to endure bravely and calmly. This ties in closely with the concept of hope that we just read about. Our hope is in God, which makes it possible for us to endure trials with grace.

Now that we have done the hard work of learning the theory behind the meaning of agape love, where does that leave us? A bit more educated, hopefully!

The question is: Are we practically equipped to start walking in this kind of love? God's kind of love is so great, so all-encompassing and so merciful and we fall so short. I just want to remind you that He would never command us to do something that is beyond our ability as Holy Spirit-filled children of God to do.

Philippians 4 v 13 reminds us:

I can do all things through Christ who strengthens me.

The "all things" that Paul mentioned in this Scripture includes loving with God's kind of Agape love!

In the next chapters, we are going to look at how to do this practically in all the different areas of our lives. I really hope you will stick with me on this journey as we seek to be transformed more and more into the image of Love Himself.

CHAPTER
Four

Agape Love in Marriage

Divine love (agape) originates from God Himself and is able to
radically transform relationships – Ken Boa

WHEN SPEAKING ABOUT MARRIAGE, I THINK WE HAVE TO first acknowledge the different roles of men and women, not only within the context of marriage, but also in society. Most of you reading this book will have been exposed to the idea of "women's lib". This movement was born during a time period when women were being subjugated and having their rights as members of society restricted. Women were not allowed to own property, speak in public, vote in elections, wear trousers, or use birth control. And that's just to name a few of the restrictions. The Women's Liberation Movement (birthed in the 1840's) sought to free women from these constraints and allow them equal opportunity alongside men. To be fair, the oppression of women has been happening all through history, as far back as there is record.

If we look at society in Jesus' days, it was just as bad. Women were second class citizens who were considered the property of their husbands or fathers. In many cultures, even today, a male family member could beat and even kill a woman with absolutely no legal consequences.

I have no doubt that every person reading this will be shocked and stirred with outrage at the treatment that some women have had to endure at the hands of men. I do believe that the oppression of women that has happened throughout history is nothing more than a well-executed plan of the enemy. He knows the power of a woman and that, without her, man is incomplete. God created men and women to complement each other and to complete each other. Satan knows that God's plan is for man and woman to stand side-by-side, on equal footing, each wielding his or her own unique power. When men and women in the Kingdom of God stand united, the devil will have a very hard time.

Unfortunately, where such an imbalance has existed for so long, when the pendulum eventually swings back, it swings back to the opposite extreme. The women's lib movement demands equality between men and women in every single aspect and this is just not how God designed us. Many women in today's modern world spend their whole lives striving to achieve in order to prove themselves equal. In many cases, the result is a life of frustration and unhappiness because women are not embracing who God created them to be, but rather trying to be like the men in their workplaces and homes.

Before you all come after me, I am not saying that women cannot do certain jobs as well as men can or achieve many of the same things as men.

I am saying that we will never *be* the same as men. We may be able to do some of the same things, but we will be more successful when we do them using the unique gifts and qualities that God placed within us. God created men to be protectors and providers, with stronger bodies, and minds focused on practicality and preparing for the future. Women were uniquely designed to be nurturers, with an unlimited capacity to love and create. Our bodies may be weaker in terms of raw strength, but we have the ability to create and sustain life within us! That's an amazing superpower!

When I was young, I considered myself a liberated woman and fought very hard in the corporate world to be taken seriously and to be seen as equal to my male colleagues. The problem was that this viewpoint spilled over into my marriage and my home life. During pre-marital counselling with the minister of the Methodist Church where my husband Andrew and I were married in 1999, we were given a copy of the standard marriage vows that we would be asked to recite. This was before the days of writing your own vows! I was totally horrified to read the vows because, where my husband had to promise to "love, honour and cherish", I was required to promise to "love, honour and obey"! The women's libber in me immediately jumped up and down in indignation and told the bewildered minister that I refused to say those words because I will not promise to obey my husband! I don't know what my poor husband-to-be thought! He probably wondered if he was making a big mistake! And no – I did not have a change of heart before the ceremony. My vows to my husband on our wedding day did not contain the word "obey".

It saddens me that so many young Christian women enter into marriage without having been taught what it actually means to be a godly woman and a godly wife. The Bible tells women to submit to their husbands. I always found this idea to be very scary and thought it meant that I would be giving away all power and control. It was not until many years later that I learned what submission in marriage really means. And let me tell you – submission in a Godly marriage is a safe place for a woman. But more about that later!

Let's have a look at what the Bible says about marriage and relationships. Ephesians 5 v 21 (under the heading of "Instructions for Christian households) says:

Submit to one another out of reverence for Christ.

It is clear from this Scripture that submission is not a one-sided thing. In modern society, the word "submission" has such a negative connotation, with most people equating it to some form of oppression. Let's have a look at what the word "submission" actually means in the ancient Greek language.

The Greek word used here is "hypotassō" [Strongs 5293] and translates as "to be subject to in an orderly fashion" or "to yield to someone's admonition or advice".

Ephesians 5 v 22 – 33 says:

Wives, submit yourselves to your own husbands as you do to the Lord. For the husband is the head of the wife as Christ is the head of the church, his body, of which he is the Savior. Now as the church submits to Christ, so also wives should submit to their husbands in everything.

Husbands, love your wives, just as Christ loved the church and gave himself up for her to make her holy, cleansing her by the washing with water through the word, and to present her to himself as a radiant church, without stain or wrinkle or any other blemish, but holy and blameless. In this same way, husbands ought to love their wives as their own bodies. He who loves his wife loves himself. After all, no one ever hated their own body, but they feed and care for their body, just as Christ does the church— for we are members of his body. "For this reason a man will leave his father and mother and be united to his wife, and the two will become one flesh." This is a profound mystery—but I am talking about Christ and the church. However, each one of you also must love his wife as he loves himself, and the wife must respect her husband.

Paul immediately dispels any notion that women are inferior or subject to men. He does not tell women to submit to men in general, but he specifically tells wives to submit to their *own* husbands. The submission of a woman to a man is meant to be practiced within the context of a godly marriage and the reason for this will become clearer as we explore God's design for marriage. If you are a woman reading this and you are already feeling a bit offended, bear with me! I am hoping that by the end of this chapter you will come to a place of understanding like I did!

The key to God's plan for marriage starts with the role of the husband. Throughout this passage, the marriage relationship is compared to Christ's relationship with the church, where He is the husband, and the church is His bride. In Ephesians 5 v 25, Paul instructs husbands to love their wives just as Christ loved the church and gave Himself up for her. This is the statement that changes everything! A godly husband is supposed to love his wife like Christ loves us! Christ loved us enough to die on the Cross for us, therefore a husband's love for his wife should be a sacrificial and selfless love. It should be a love which only sees the best and hopes for the best.

Is Christ's love for His church controlling? Is it oppressive? Is it abusive? Is it rude? Is it violent? Obviously, the answer to all these questions is a resounding "No!" Christ's love is the unconditional, agape love that we learned about in the previous chapter.

When a husband loves his wife with God's kind of love, seeking only the best for her and putting his own needs and desires second, then a wife has no need to come into conflict with her husband. It is in this space that a wife can feel safe because she is cared for and provided for. As women, what we desire most is love and affection (the outward display of love). This is why Paul commands in Ephesians 5 v 25:

Husbands, love your wives.

When love is freely and unconditionally given, it allows us as women to step into our God-given purpose with confidence. Whether we are full time homemakers, teachers, executives, politicians or businesswomen, a wife needs the love and support of her husband in order to reach her full potential. Please note that I am not speaking to single women or saying that a woman needs a man to succeed in life! I am speaking specifically of married women. As soon as a woman enters the covenant of marriage, she is no longer just herself, but becomes one with her husband. No partner in a marriage can function properly without the other.

Ephesians 5 v 33 says:

Nevertheless let each one of you in particular so love his own wife as himself, and let the wife see that she respects her husband.

Men were created with an innate need for respect. Marriage expert and researcher Shaunti Feldhahn says: "A man's highest need is to feel respect, whereas a woman's highest need is to feel loved." It is important for women to understand this about men so that they can start to affirm their husbands in a way that is meaningful to them. Men need to feel respected in their knowledge, abilities, opinions, and decisions. Many men feel like their wives question their decisions and argue with them instead of trusting their judgement.

This once again highlights the reciprocal relationship of agape love. If a husband is loving his wife the way he should, she will trust his judgement and defer to him when it is appropriate. This does not mean that the husband gets to dictate to the wife – marriage is a partnership, which means that decisions should be made collaboratively. Sometimes, however, a final call must be made and in a godly marriage, that responsibility falls to the husband. This is true submission – willingly allowing someone to make a decision that affects you, knowing that they have your best interests at heart and will ultimately make a choice that will benefit you.

If you are a wife and you are reading this, I hope that the concept of submission is starting to sound more like a warm, safe place to you than a type of oppression. It is all about understanding God's heart for marriage. He is a loving Father and He would not want any person to be in an oppressive or controlling relationship.

Something that often comes up when speaking to people about their marriages is that they seem one-sided. Many times, one of the partners will feel like they are making all the effort and getting nothing back in return. What often happens is they become frustrated and give up trying, which results in even more distance in the marriage. If we are going to approach the marriage relationship in the flesh, it will always be about "me" and "What can I get out of it?" It will always be focused on what my partner does wrong or doesn't do right! When we approach our marriages with the nature of agape love, it suddenly becomes more about how we can serve our partners and help them to become everything God has created them to be.

Now we need to look at what this all means practically. Otherwise, what's the use, right?

Let's briefly remind ourselves again of what love is (taken from The Message Bible):

Love never gives up.
Love cares more for others than for self.
Love doesn't want what it doesn't have.
Love doesn't strut,
Doesn't have a swelled head,

Doesn't force itself on others,
Isn't always "me first",
Doesn't fly off the handle,
Doesn't keep score of the sins of others,
Doesn't revel when others grovel,
Takes pleasure in the flowering of truth,
Puts up with anything,
Trusts God always,
Always looks for the best,
Never looks back,
But keeps going to the end.

If you think back about your interactions with your spouse over the past week, or even the past 24 hours, how do you score against the list above? If I am being honest, I would have to say not very well! Some days I do better than other days, and I'm sure you can say the same! This should not make us feel bad about ourselves or make us feel condemned. Agape love is a godly standard that we may never attain, but we should certainly strive to follow Jesus' example of love whenever and wherever possible.

Let's wrap up this chapter with a few practical ideas of how we can show agape love to our spouses. I challenge every person reading this to try at least one of these things for a week and see what a difference it makes in your marriage.

1.   Choose forgiveness.

   1 Corinthians 13 v 5 says that love thinks no evil. Another way of putting it is that love keeps no record of wrongs. I'm sure you have

experienced during an argument how quick we are to bring up what our spouse did wrong five or even ten years ago! This definitely qualifies as keeping record of wrongs! We need to choose to forgive, and that means not dredging up the past! Choose this week to walk in forgiveness when dealing with your spouse. After all, next week you might be the one in need of forgiveness!

2. Put your spouse's needs before your own.
    Sacrifice and love go hand in hand. If we truly love someone, we will not be selfish when they need something. Surprise your partner this week by allowing their needs to take preference, even when it inconveniences you. Agape love requires us to be intentional and to make an effort.

3. Serve your spouse without expecting anything in return.
    Often we are willing to do things for each other when we know it will be reciprocated somehow. Genuine love allows us to serve without any expectation – simply to please or benefit the person we are serving. Get up and make that cup of coffee or go and run that bubble bath…just because it will bless your partner.

CHAPTER
Five

Agape Love in the Family

What you do in your house is worth as much as if you did it up in heaven for our Lord God – Martin Luther

W E HAVE ALL HEARD THE EXPRESSION "YOU CAN CHOOSE your friends, but you can't choose your family." Whilst this is often said in a joking way, the reality is that strife within the family is a daily occurrence in many households. In fact, in my experience of dealing with people, family members often treat each other worse than they would ever treat strangers. Make no mistake; this is not limited to non-Christians. This happens every single day in Christian households. The very structure of the family is under attack, and relationships between parents and children, brothers and sisters, grandparents and grandchildren are the unfortunate casualties of this insidious war.

Satan's strategy is always to seek to destroy relationships and, when aimed at the family, this attacks the very heart of the nature of Father God. God's heart is relational. Not only did He create man so that He could have fellowship with us and enjoy us (Revelation 4 v 11), but He was prepared to sacrifice His own Son to restore that relationship after sin destroyed it. Even the way He teaches us to relate to Him in the Scriptures shows us His heart for family and relationship.

In 2 Corinthians 6 v 18 it says:

'I will be a Father to you, and you shall be My sons and daughters,' says the Lord Almighty.

The Scriptures also tell us:

Behold what manner of love the Father has bestowed on us, that we should be called children of God!

1 John 3 v 1

He calls Himself our Father, and us His sons and daughters! What an amazing privilege to be part of God's family!

Even though this chapter will primarily deal with the relationship between parents and children, it is beneficial that we spend a bit of time looking at how the breakdown of the family structure, over the last few decades especially, has had a significant impact on the values and morals in society. The so-called First World countries have seen a noticeable decline in traditional family values and a resulting lowering of moral standards in society and government.

Consider the following facts and statistics:

- Marriage has become increasingly unfashionable. In 1980, the percentage of babies born in the USA to unmarried mothers was 18.4%, compared to 40% in 2020.
- Entertainment media (music, television, movies) and print media all present sex outside marriage as an acceptable cultural norm.
- Pornography, which defiles the beautiful image of intimacy within godly marriage, has become so widely accepted that one study reports that 55% of married men watch pornography at least once a month.
- Welfare policies in many countries provide more benefits to single parent families than to married couples, in a sense providing incentive for couples not to marry.
- Roe vs Wade, 410 U.S. 113 (1973) ruled that it is a woman's "right" to end the life of her unborn child. According to the Guttmacher Institute, an estimated 930 160 abortions took place in the United States in 2020. This means that approximately 20% of all pregnancies in the USA in 2020 (excluding miscarriages) ended in abortion. In 2020, unmarried women accounted for 86% of all abortions in the USA.
- Addiction and its effect on families is difficult to quantify. But these days it is safe to say that the majority of families have been negatively impacted in some way by alcohol, drug, gambling, or other addictions.

This might sound like a strange thing to say, but I hope that these facts scare you as much as they scare me. The worst thing that can happen is that we become desensitized to what is happening around us. We cannot afford to compromise simply because it's the easy road to take. We must push back against the pressure from the world to conform to non-biblical practices and make sure that we restore the family, and society in general, to what God intended it to be.

It is the Christ-centred family that produces children who are emotionally and psychologically equipped to deal with the pressures of living in today's world. It is the Christ-centred family that produces children who serve the Lord. It is the Christ-centred family that raises ethical business leaders, politicians who lead with integrity and employees who work with a spirit of excellence. A moral society is built on the foundation of God's design for the family. If Satan is allowed to destroy the biblical family, then society and culture starts to collapse.

Let's get back to the topic of love within the family. There is no disputing that family was important to Jesus. In fact, it was one of the last things on His mind before He died on the Cross.

In John 19 v 26 – 27, we read:

When Jesus therefore saw His mother, and the disciple whom He loved standing by, He said to His mother, "Woman, behold your son!" Then He said to the disciple, "Behold your mother!" And from that hour that disciple took her to his own home.

One of His last acts as a human was to ensure that His mother would be taken care of. If you stop and think about the enormity of the situation and what was happening, would you not have expected His final words to be some words of wisdom or instruction directed at His disciples? After all, they were the ones to whom He was entrusting His Gospel and His ministry. Maybe some last-minute directions about the way forward? Maybe some tips about building His church? However, in that moment His agape love for His mother superseded all else and His priority was to make sure that she would have a home and a family after He was gone. This speaks a great deal about the importance Jesus placed on family.

There are many different types of relationships within families, but let's start off by talking about the relationship between parents and children.

Loving your *Children* God's Way

One of the easiest ways that we can get a glimpse of what God's love for us is like is when we become parents. Most of us, I would like to think, love our children unconditionally and would literally give our lives for them. I know from my own experience that no matter what my children do or how angry they make me, it doesn't stop me from loving them or make me love them any less. If you are a parent, I am sure you have looked into a feverish, tear-stained little face and wished that you could take the pain and sickness on yourself. Why is that? It's because when you love someone selflessly, you would rather suffer than see them suffer. Isn't that exactly what Jesus did for us when He died on the Cross? He took our sin and sickness upon Himself so that we do not have to suffer the consequences.

We have an advantage because we can look back and see God's plan for His children in the context of the finished work of Jesus on the Cross. We can see the Father's love for us in action. Think for a moment of what it must have been like for the Jewish people in Jesus' time. They had lived for centuries under the Law of Moses. They knew God was their God and they were His chosen people, but they had to obey a very long and very strict set of laws in order to please God. We know from the events recorded in the Old Testament that this was, in practice, an impossibility. We also now know that the whole purpose of the Law was to show us that we can never be righteous through our own efforts and that we desperately need a Saviour. I am sure that the majority of the Jewish people of that time were fearful of displeasing God and had absolutely no concept of Him as a loving Father. They had no idea that this Teacher, Jesus, was the physical expression of God's love for them and that they were about to witness the ultimate act of agape love.

When Jesus shared the Good News of what He had come to do, He had to find a way to change people's perception of the nature of God. He often taught in parables because they helped to explain difficult concepts using imagery that was familiar to the people. Jesus used the parable of the Prodigal Son to try and explain the simplicity of God's love for His children. I use the word "simplicity" on purpose because it is just that. Nothing we do or don't do can make Him love us any more or any less. It's so simple. God loves you. Forget the rules, the sacrifices, the rituals, the dress code, the feasts, the festivals. God loves you and you can't change that.

There are also lessons for us as Christian parents in this portion of Scripture about how we should love our children with God's kind of love. We read in Luke 15 v 11 – 24:

Then He said: A certain man had two sons. And the younger of them said to his father, "Father, give me the portion of goods that falls to me." So he divided to them his livelihood. And not many days after, the younger son gathered all together, journeyed to a far country, and there wasted his possessions with prodigal living. But when he had spent all, there arose a severe famine in that land, and he began to be in want. Then he went and joined himself to a citizen of that country, and he sent him into his fields to feed swine. And he would gladly have filled his stomach with the pods that the swine ate, and no one gave him anything.

But when he came to himself, he said, "How many of my father's hired servants have bread enough and to spare, and I perish with hunger! I will arise and go to my father, and will say to him, 'Father, I have sinned against heaven and before you, and I am no longer worthy to be called your son. Make me like one of your hired servants.'"

And he arose and came to his father. But when he was still a great way off, his father saw him and had compassion, and ran and fell on his neck and kissed him. And the son said to him, "Father, I have sinned against heaven and in your sight, and am no longer worthy to be called your son."

But the father said to his servants, "Bring out the best robe and put it on him, and put a ring on his hand and sandals on his feet. And bring the fatted calf here and kill it, and let us eat and be merry; for this my son was dead and is alive again; he was lost and is found." And they began to be merry.

Jesus told this parable to try and help people to understand how God the Father loves us. As in all aspects of life, He is the perfect example. We can take this blueprint of a father operating in agape love towards his son and apply it in our own lives. Please remember that this is not meant to be a lesson in parenting, but rather a reminder of how we can show God's kind of love to our children.

There are three important things we can take away from the Parable of the Prodigal Son :

1. Children need unconditional love.

    We learned in the previous chapters that God's kind of love is unconditional. The father in the parable welcomed his son with compassion, affection, and open arms, not words of blame, judgement, or ridicule. The son knew very well that he deserved an "I told you so!" and had even rehearsed an apology for his behaviour. How many Christian parents have rejected their children for making stupid decisions? How often do we feel the need to lecture our children about their mistakes when they come to us for help? This is not God's kind of love. We must ensure that when our children feel lost and helpless, they can turn to us and find grace and compassion, not condemnation.

    It is also important that we are not prideful when our children make mistakes. We are often so worried about our reputation or what others will say, that we sometimes try and sweep issues under the carpet. This teaches our children that a mistake is something shameful, when in fact we should teach them to celebrate the lesson that has been learned and the good decisions that were made. In the parable, the father celebrated his son's decision to return home where he belonged.

2. Children need freedom to fail.
This statement might shock you, but it is a truth that parents should not ignore. While it is one of our primary roles as parents to protect our children, we also must allow them to learn that decisions and actions have consequences. The father of the prodigal son knew that his son was making a mistake. The Scriptures clearly state that receiving an inheritance while the person is still alive is not right. (Hebrews 9 v 17 and Proverbs 20 v 21). He knew that his son was being motivated by lust and sin and that he would ultimately end up in a bad situation. For a Jewish boy to end up tending pigs and even considering eating their food really represented hitting rock bottom in life. Despite this, the father chose to let his son go his own way. Did he write him off? No, definitely not!
In verse 20 it says:

But when he was still a great way off, his father saw him and had compassion, and ran and fell on his neck and kissed him.

The mere fact that he saw his son coming from a long way off tells us that the father was watching, hoping, praying, and expecting his son to return. It is interesting to note that he did not go out and look for his son to bring him back home. He resisted the urge to "rescue" him and allowed him the freedom to decide to come back on his own. Imagine how difficult this must have been! This is where we need the Holy Spirit to guide us and give us wisdom and discernment in every situation we face as parents!

3. Children need grace.

Grace is often defined in biblical terms as undeserved favour or kindness. We always tend to equate favour or reward with our performance, and we struggle with the concept of receiving good things when we didn't earn them. The school system, the workplace, and society in general reinforces the concept that you must perform in order to be rewarded. This makes it difficult for many people later in life to receive from God. The Bible tells us in Romans that salvation and eternal life are free gifts from God. We need to model grace for our children so that one day when they meet Jesus, they will be able to freely accept the undeserved gift He offers to each one of us.

In the Parable of the Prodigal Son, the father extends grace to his son when he returns home. Even in the son's mind, he deserved nothing more than to be treated like one of the hired servants. Despite what he deserved, his father immediately restored him to his prior status by clothing him in fine robes, putting a ring on his finger and throwing him a party! What amazing grace!

We can either model the concept of agape love for our children or give them a distorted perception of what love should be. Many Christians struggle as adults to relate to God the Father as a loving parent because of the example their human parents set. So often, when I have spoken with people who struggle to receive from God and cannot accept the infinite depths of His love for them, they admit that they had a broken or dysfunctional relationship with their father growing up. This seems to be a pattern that reveals itself over and over again. People who had abusive and angry fathers tend to see God as harsh and punitive, while people whose fathers were distant or absent often feel that God does not care about them or their daily struggles.

There is something we haven't addressed yet in terms of the parent-child relationship, and that is discipline. Loving our children unconditionally and showing them grace does not mean that they are never going to need correction. As with most things, it is how we do it and our heart behind it that matters. Part of our responsibility as parents is to discipline our children, but it needs to be balanced with love and encouragement.

The Bible tells us in Colossians 3 v 21:

Fathers, do not provoke your children, lest they become discouraged.

Discouragement, and the perception that they can never do anything right, can often drive children in the opposite direction to which they should go. When Father God corrects us, it is never harsh or punitive – it is always gentle and loving because agape love always seeks the best for others. Even in discipline, love can shine through because the character and long-term welfare of a child is more important than making them happy in the short term.

In every interaction with our children, we should be striving to mirror the loving heart of God. This way, once they are introduced to Him as their Father, they will be able to fall into His arms with a sigh of relief, knowing beyond all doubt that He will always take care of them.

Psalm 127 v 3 tells us:

Children are a gift from the Lord; they are a reward from Him.

We need to make sure that we cherish and care for these precious gifts so that when the time is right, we can safely entrust them to His care.

Loving your *Parents* God's Way

Children also have responsibilities in this relationship. The Bible clearly tells us in Ephesians 6 v 1 - 3:

Children, obey your parents in the Lord, for this is right. 'Honor your father and mother,' which is the first commandment with promise: 'that it may be well with you and you may live long on the earth.'

Young children honour their father and mother through their obedience and respect, but as adults, honouring our parents will look a bit different. When we leave our parents' home, start busy careers, get married, and have our own children, it is easy to forget about the responsibility we still have towards our parents. The busy-ness of life and the frantic pace of the world in which we live leaves little time for anything outside our immediate circle of focus. This doesn't change the fact that we are still required to honour our parents and act in agape love towards them.

Tim Keller says: "It's respect for your parents that is the basis for every other kind of respect and every other kind of authority."

Honouring our mother and father is part of submitting to authority, which the Bible speaks about in Romans 13 v 7. What many of us don't realise is that this does not only apply to when we are living under our parents' roof. The debt of honour we owe our parents continues long after that. As in all relationships, there will be times when it is extremely difficult to operate in God's kind of love. Relationships between adult children and their parents can be volatile! Remember the definition of love in 1 Corinthians 13? We need to treat our parents with patience, kindness, forgiveness, and respect. And the part we sometimes forget – we need to seek their good above our own.

Here are 3 practical ways we can honour our parents:

1. Forgive them.

    Showing forgiveness towards parents is something that a lot of people struggle with as adults. The fact is that there is no perfect parent besides Father God. Our earthly parents have all made mistakes, said hurtful things, had unrealistic expectations and in severe cases, neglected and even abused us. Many people go through life carrying a lot of anger and bitterness towards their parents. I know this is easier said than done, but if we are to imitate Love Himself, we need to come to a place where we can extend grace and forgiveness towards our parents. If you find yourself unable to forgive one or both of your parents for past hurts or mistakes, I encourage you to ask the Holy Spirit to help you to deal with those hurts. He is always faithful and will walk the road to freedom and forgiveness by your side.

2. Support them.

As children and adolescents, we longed for freedom and independence. Our parents raised us and equipped us to be able to leave home and stand on our own. There comes a time though, as our parents age, that they become physically weaker and less independent. In essence, the ones who cared for and protected us become the ones in need of care and protection. So many elderly people fear being alone, neglected and physically unable to care for themselves. Even David voiced this fear to the Lord in Psalm 71 v 9. He said:

Do not cast me off in the time of old age; Do not forsake me when my strength fails.

We can honour our parents by giving them the assurance that we will not neglect them in their old age. It is our responsibility to care for them as they cared for us. The problem in today's society (most predominantly in western culture) is that some children seem to think that providing for parents financially in terms of old age housing and nursing care is where their responsibility ends.

So many elderly people are living in institutions cared for by strangers instead of family members. Children visit reluctantly out of obligation once a month or on special occasions. As children of God, we have a responsibility to love our parents the way He loves us. Agape love is hands-on and practical and there is no justification for the emotional neglect and abandonment that many elderly people face.

3.   Value their advice.
Wisdom is with aged men, and with length of days, understanding.

Job 12 v 12

The Scriptures tell us that wisdom and understanding come with age. We can honour our parents by asking for their advice when we are facing difficulties or major decisions. This does not mean that we always have to follow the advice that they offer but, when we seek their input, we are in essence placing value and worth in their years of accumulated experience. Just because their bodies may be failing them does not mean that they have nothing to offer. It is a biblical principle for younger people to learn from their elders. Proverbs 13 v 1 says:

A wise son heeds his father's instruction, but a scoffer does not listen to rebuke.

Knowing that Jesus placed such value on family and relationships, I hope that this chapter inspires you to be mindful of how you relate to your immediate family. When we share the same space as people, the old saying of "familiarity breeds contempt" often holds true. It is very easy to become irritated and annoyed with the people we live with, and unfortunately our family members often bear the brunt of our negative emotions and stress. Whether dealing with parents, siblings, or children, my prayer is that you allow Jesus to be your example and your guide.

CHAPTER
Six

Agape Love in the Church

*It's easy to talk about how much you love God, but loving others
reveals how much you truly do. – Elizabeth George*

L OVE SHOULD CHARACTERISE THE CHURCH. I REALISE IT MAY
sound like I am stating the obvious, but is that the reality in most
churches today? Sadly, the answer is no. If you get to the end of this chapter
and don't feel a little rubbed up the wrong way, then I won't have achieved
my goal. Yes, I am going to point fingers at the church, not for the purpose
of breaking down, but rather to help us to see where we can do things
better. The process of acknowledging where we fall short can be an
uncomfortable one, but sometimes our mindset and the way we do things
needs to be challenged in order for us to grow and move forward.

Let's first make sure we all understand what "church" is. People have so
many different expectations and experiences of church. For many, church
is simply a building where they go for an hour or two a week to sing a few
songs and listen to a sermon. For others, church is wherever believers
gather in the name of Jesus, whether in homes, schools, or workplaces.

I think its important to differentiate between the church as a family of believers versus the physical building where people meet. Yes, that is what we call the building, but that wasn't what Jesus spoke about when He spoke about the church.

In 1 Corinthians 12 v 13, Paul says:

For by one Spirit we were all baptized into one body—whether Jews or Greeks, whether slaves or free—and have all been made to drink into one Spirit. For in fact the body is not one member but many.

Then in Colossians 1 v 18 we read:

And He is the head of the body, the church, who is the beginning, the firstborn from the dead, that in all things He may have the preeminence.

From these two Scriptures, we can see that the body of Christ and the Church are one and the same. When we accept Jesus as Lord and Saviour and are born again, we are baptised into the body of Christ which comprises all those who believe in Him. We are all members of the global church or body of believers.

Going forward, when we talk about church I will largely be referring to the local church or smaller group of believers that meet for fellowship on a regular basis. You might be part of mega church of a thousand people or a house church of 15 people – they are both churches.

Whatever form church takes for you, what characterises it is people. You can be sure that wherever people of different ages, genders, races, and cultures come together, even around a common belief, there will be personality clashes, strife, and conflict. This is not God's heart and I believe that the division and hurt experienced by many of His children in churches causes Him great sadness. There are so many Scriptures that talk about how He wants His children to relate to each other, yet this is an area where few of us succeed. In this chapter, we will explore what it says in the Bible about how believers should treat each other, bearing in mind that we should be the image bearers of agape love as described in 1 Corinthians 13.

There is a song that I love called "Church (Take Me Back)" by Cochren & Co. If you don't know it, I would encourage you to listen to it. This song epitomises for me how I think we ought to feel about church. The chorus of the song goes as follows:

"Take me back
To the place that feels like home
To the people I can depend on
To the faith that's in my bones
Take me back
To a preacher and a verse
Where they've seen me at my worst
To the love I had at first
Oh, I want to go to church."

I believe that church is meant to be a home, a place of refuge and acceptance. I, personally, have been lucky enough to experience being part of a church family that felt like just that – a family. I looked forward with anticipation to church meetings because I loved being there and spending time with the people. There was no greater joy for me than to worship the

Lord and explore His Word with my brothers and sisters in Christ. We were part of each other's lives and I experienced genuine love and acceptance in that church.

Unfortunately, this is not every person's experience of church. More people than I can count have told me how they experienced hurt, judgement and rejection in the church. The saddest part of all is that many of those people have never and will never set foot in a church again. They will often say "It doesn't matter - I don't need to go to church to be a Christian." While that is fundamentally true, they are missing out on an integral part of being a member of God's family. We do not need to belong to a church to please God or to go to Heaven, but we need the fellowship, teaching, edification, encouragement and equipping that comes from believers seeking the Lord together.

The Scriptures tell us in Hebrews 10 v 24-25:

And let us consider one another in order to stir up love and good works, not forsaking the assembling of ourselves together, as is the manner of some, but exhorting one another, and so much more as you see the Day approaching.

These verses tell us that gathering with other believers is becoming even *more* important as Jesus' return draws nearer. There is danger in trying to live the Christian life in isolation. To name a few reasons:

- Discouragement, doubt, and depression multiply when we do not have others to encourage us, lift us up, and share our burdens. (Galatians 6 v 2)

- We have all been given spiritual gifts to use for the edification of the Body of Christ, and if we are not gathering with others, we may miss the opportunity to develop and exercise these gifts and to bless others with them. (1 Peter 4 v 10 – 11)
- The church is the place from which we are sent out into the world, equipped and empowered. (Ephesians 4 v 11-12)

There is no doubt in my mind that Jesus' heart for us as His children is for us to gather together as family, to love each other with His kind of love and to help each other wherever possible. I'm sure we all understand that we are ambassadors for Jesus in the world, but sometimes we forget that this applies in the church as well. This is especially applicable to church leaders. Those in leadership don't always realise how greatly they can affect someone's view of God, either positively or negatively. If God's chosen leaders treat the people in their care without love, what does that say about the God they serve?

In James 3 v 1, it tells us that those who teach in the church will be judged more strictly. The reason for this is because of the greater amount of influence that leaders have over the people they aspire to lead. When a leader falls, they have the potential to take many people down with them and, for this reason, leaders will be held accountable for the impact that they have on the people entrusted to them. That said – there is no perfect church and there are no perfect leaders. People are fundamentally flawed by nature, but we still need to strive to operate in God's kind of love within the church environment.

At the beginning of this chapter, I made the statement that love should characterise the church. The following Scripture is a bombshell that should blow many of us right out of the water of our own self-righteousness.

By this all will know that you are My disciples, if you have love for one another.

John 13 v 35

Does your love for your fellow Christians, particularly those in your church, make people stop and wonder what is different about you? According to the Scripture above, it should! Our love for one another should be such a blazing beacon of light that people should know immediately that we are followers of Jesus Christ. His nature should so characterise our actions and interactions that the world only sees Jesus and we fade into the background. It's a tall order, I know. But it is one we need to strive to fulfil.

There are certain stumbling blocks to walking in love in the church environment. I am sure that many of us who have been involved in churches have experienced these to some degree. The two most obvious ones are judgement and offense.

Let's talk about judgement first. There is a quote by Mother Theresa that I love. She said:

"If you judge people, you have no time to love them."

How true this is. Judgement so often interferes with our relationships and our ability to connect with one another. Stop and think about it. Generally, before you have even met someone, you have already formed an opinion or judgement about them based on how they look or what you have heard about them. This is a very shallow example of judgement, but one we all understand. Obviously judgement runs much deeper than this. What I am trying to illustrate is that we need to take the time to set aside our perceptions so that we can love the person based on who Christ created them to be rather than based on our own standards.

When we "do life" with other Christians, it is natural that we will not agree with one another's actions all the time. Every single one of us is flawed, and circumstances can sometimes cause us to behave in ways that are hurtful or unfair towards others. It's not wrong to judge that someone's actions are offensive or incorrect, but we need to be very careful not to judge *why* they behaved that way. Discerning the motivation of people's hearts is best left to God because only He can truly know us on that level. If we could relate to each other on a heart level, we would be a lot more compassionate and understanding. On most occasions when we are hurt or wronged by someone, it has nothing to do with us and everything to do with pain or hardship in the other person's life.

It is important to understand that there are different types of judgement. The Bible does not say we must never judge. There is a place for it, particularly when it comes to the issue of church discipline, but even then it is not something that should be done lightly by church leaders.

There are Scriptures where both Jesus and the disciples told people that they *should* judge, but in many instances, the word "discern" was used interchangeably with the word "judge". It is right that we use discernment, aided by the Holy Spirit, to appraise people and situations. It is when judgement results in condemnation that it becomes a major stumbling block to love within the body of Christ.

Jesus warns us very clearly in Matthew 7 v 1-5 about judgement. He says:

Judge not, that you be not judged. For with what judgment you judge, you will be judged; and with the measure you use, it will be measured back to you. And why do you look at the speck in your brother's eye, but do not consider the plank in your own eye? Or how can you say to your brother, 'Let me remove the speck from your eye'; and look, a plank is in your own eye? Hypocrite! First remove the plank from your own eye, and then you will see clearly to remove the speck from your brother's eye.

Jesus is telling us in no uncertain terms that how we treat each other is important. If we treat each other harshly, people will tend to retaliate and be harsh towards us. According to the principle of sowing and reaping, we should treat people the way we would like to be treated. Jesus goes on to illustrate the importance of judging ourselves first before judging others. Much of the conflict and hurt we experience in the church could be avoided if we followed this principle. If we look honestly at our own shortcomings, we will be far less hasty to judge what we perceive to be flaws in other people. Often, when we find something offensive in someone else, we are guilty of the very same thing. Self-examination makes us much *less* likely to judge others and much *more* likely to show them forgiveness, compassion, and grace.

In the Merriam-Webster online dictionary, offense is defined as "the act of displeasing or affronting" or "the state of being insulted or morally outraged". The first is the act of giving offense and the second is the act of taking offense.

There is that old saying "Offense is taken, not given." In a respect, this holds true. We cannot always control what people say to us, but we can control our reaction and how we receive it. When someone insults us or treats us unkindly, we can choose whether we will take offense or not. I'm not saying it is easy to do this, but it is possible.

Let's look at an example of how Jesus reacted to what was an extremely unfair and offensive situation.

It was customary for the governor of Judea to pardon and release a convicted prisoner just before the celebration of Passover. When Pontius Pilate gave the crowd the choice between Jesus and Barabbas, a notorious convicted murderer, the crowd chose Barabbas to be pardoned. Pontius Pilate tried to reason with the crowd by reminding them that Jesus had not actually committed any crime, but it did not make them change their minds. In fact, they were so determined to see Jesus killed that in Matthew 27 v 25 they say:

His blood be on us and on our children.

They wanted Him crucified so badly that they were willing to sacrifice the lives of the next generation to see Him dead. Crazy to say the least!

Faced with such unfounded hatred and anger, what was Jesus' response? He did not get offended and try to defend Himself. He did not point out the unfairness of the situation. He did not get angry and argumentative. He did not demand an apology. He kept His eyes firmly on His Father and the task that lay before Him and did not utter a word. He did not try and get even. In fact, He redeemed those who called for His death! That is love in action!

Proverbs 19 v 11 says:

The discretion of a man makes him slow to anger, and his glory is to overlook a transgression.

When we consider the example that Jesus set, we begin to realise that we have no right to take offense when people treat us badly. Jesus withstood the ultimate offense on our behalf, so we need to do the same when faced with unfair or hurtful treatment. We need to glorify Him through our reactions by responding to perceived offense with action driven by love.

The Bible teaches us not to take offence because the long-term effects are not to our benefit. The moment we choose to be angry, we open ourselves up to bitterness, hatred and unforgiveness. In 1 John 3 v 15 it says:

Whoever hates his brother is a murderer, and you know that no murderer has eternal life abiding in him.

The results of offense can have eternal consequences, which is why we need to be so careful about how we deal with it. The best way to deal with offense is not to take it in the first place! Think of how you would react if someone tried to hand you a box of poisonous snakes or spiders! I don't know about you, but I would run in the opposite direction! We need to react the same way when offense is offered. Remember what we learned in 1 Corinthians 13 v 5? Love thinks no evil and keeps no record of wrongs. A heart rooted in God's kind of love will shrug off offense and respond with grace and kindness.

While the definition of agape love in 1 Corinthians 13 is the over-arching banner leading us on this journey, there are also many Scriptures in the New Testament that speak directly about how we, as followers of Jesus, should love each other.

Let's look at a few:

1. Give preference to one another.
   We read in Romans 12 v 10:
   Be kindly affectionate to one another with brotherly love, in honor giving preference to one another .

   In this Scripture, Paul references "phileo" which is brotherly love or tender affection. "Kindly affection" was translated from the Greek word "philostorgos" which means "cherishing one's kindred". In the last part of this verse, he speaks of giving preference to one another, which is the same as putting the other person's needs before our own – a characteristic of agape love. Are you tender and affectionate to the people in your church? Do you cherish them as your family? Do you put their needs before your own?

2. Be part of one another's lives.

Romans 12 v 15 says:

Rejoice with those who rejoice, and weep with those who weep.

This Scripture speaks once again of putting others before ourselves. If we are self-centered we will not be able to rejoice with others because jealousy will get in the way. Remember – love does not envy. Similarly, a self-centered person cannot operate in compassion to feel someone else's sorrow. This verse is in essence telling us to do life together. We need to be aware of what others are going through so that we can celebrate with them in good times and support them during difficult times.

3. Bear one another's burdens.

Galatians 6 v 2 tells us :

Bear one another's burdens, and so fulfil the law of Christ.

The Greek word that was translated as "burdens" in this verse is "baros". It literally means a weight so heavy that if the person did not receive help, they would be unable to bear it. This brings to mind Simon the Cyrene helping Jesus to carry His cross when He did not have the strength anymore.

If we are to fulfil the law of Christ which commands us to love our neighbour, we must make the leap from intention to action.

Feeling sorry for a brother who is carrying a heavy burden is not enough. We need to take action to alleviate their suffering if it is within our power to do so.

4. Show compassion, kindness, and forgiveness to one another.
   It says in Ephesians 4 v 32:

   And be kind to one another, tenderhearted, forgiving one another, even as God in Christ forgave you.

   Here we see a reiteration of the qualities of the kind of love we are called to show each other. Kindness, compassion, and forgiveness should be woven into our godly relationships.

5. Choose the spirit, not the flesh.
   Colossians 3 v 12 - 14 says:

   Therefore, as the elect of God, holy and beloved, put on tender mercies, kindness, humility, meekness, longsuffering; bearing with one another, and forgiving one another, if anyone has a complaint against another; even as Christ forgave you, so you also must do. But above all these things put on love, which is the bond of perfection.

   Once again, we see most of the qualities of agape love being described in this Scripture. Paul had just been speaking about the "old man" vs the "new man" and is highlighting here that we need to operate in love towards one another out of the spirit, not the flesh. Agape love is love born of the spirit.

6. Love one another fervently.

We read in 1 Peter 4 v 8-9:

And above all things have fervent love for one another, for 'love will cover a multitude of sins'. Be hospitable to one another without grumbling.

This verse references Proverbs 10 v 12 which says:

Hatred stirs up strife, but love covers all sins.

Every single one of us has sin that needs covering. We need to love each other through the lens of God's kind of love, which does not see our sins. Remember – agape love forgives and holds no record of wrongs. We need to offer the same grace to each other that Jesus offered to us. We need to love each other not because we are lovely, but rather because Jesus has told us to do so. The other notable thing in this verse is the word "fervent". It was translated from the Greek word "ektenes" which was also used in Acts 12 v 5. It was translated as "without ceasing". We need to love each other without ceasing and not give up when things get hard.

7. Love one another sacrificially.

It says in 1 John 3 v 16:

By this we know love, because He laid down His life for us. And we also ought to lay down our lives for the brethren.

Here we are reminded that God's love for us was displayed in the action of Jesus laying down His life for us. Our love towards one another must result in action otherwise it is not God's kind of love. It is easy to say we love each other but not so easy to follow through with action, especially when it requires sacrifice on our part.

We can see from these few Scriptures that the Lord had very specific ideas about how He wants us to love each other.

Let's end off with some practical ways that we can show love to the people in our church family:

1. Offer words of encouragement
   Therefore comfort each other and edify one another, just as you are also doing.

   1 Thessalonians 5 v 11

   A word of encouragement can make all the difference to someone going through a difficult time. Take the time to speak to people, especially those you don't usually connect with, and find opportunities to encourage them.

2. Pray for one another
   Confess your trespasses to one another, and pray for one another, that you may be healed. The effective, fervent prayer of a righteous man avails much.

   James 5 v 16

It is important that we pray for each other, not only in our own private prayer time, but also in person. We are often reluctant to ask someone if we can pray for them, but it is not just the job of church leaders to pray for people. I never fail to be surprised and humbled by how much it means to people when you step out in obedience and pray for them.

3. Serve others with love

   If I then, your Lord and Teacher, have washed your feet, you also ought to wash one another's feet.

   John 13 v 14

Agape love is a sacrificial love. We love those around us when we do things for them without expecting anything in return. Sometimes an unexpected gesture as small as making someone a cup of coffee or buying them a chocolate can make someone feel loved and valued at the exact moment when they need it.

4. Bear each other's burdens

   Bear one another's burdens, and so fulfill the law of Christ.

   Galatians 6 v 2

So often in churches, people face terrible difficulties, and their church family does not even know about it. There is a tendency amongst Christians to "put on a happy face" because we sometimes feel ashamed or embarrassed to share our struggles. Jesus Himself said that there would be troubles in this life. The joy of following Christ is not the absence of hardship, but rather the assurance that we won't have to face difficulties alone. Life is often messy and there will be times when we will need to step in and get our hands dirty. Taking the initiative to share what you are going through can create a safe space for others to do the same.

CHAPTER
Seven

Agape Love in the Workplace

True Christianity is love in action. There is no better way to manifest love for God than to show an unselfish love for your fellow men. This is the spirit of missionary work. – David O. McKay

HAVE YOU NOTICED HOW MANY PEOPLE ARE DISMISSIVE OF the job that they do? When you meet someone for the first time and ask what they do for a living, they will often respond with "Oh, I'm just a bookkeeper," or "I'm just a teacher," or "I'm just a shop assistant."

The fact of the matter is that none of us are "just" anything! We are a bookkeeper for the Lord, a teacher for the Lord or a shop assistant for the Lord! There is a perception that if you are not in full time ministry, you are not doing the Lord's work. This misinformed mindset has led to a culture in which many Christians believe that reaching out to people is exclusively the work of ministers, missionaries, and evangelists. The truth is that the Great Commission was given to us all, irrespective of our occupation.

And Jesus came and spoke to them, saying, "All authority has been given to Me in heaven and on earth. Go therefore and make disciples of all the nations, baptizing them in the name of the Father and of the Son and of the Holy Spirit, teaching them to observe all things that I have commanded you; and lo, I am with you always, even to the end of the age.

Matthew 28 v 18 - 20

If you consider yourself to be a disciple of Jesus, then the Scripture above applies to you. And in terms of the commandment to love your neighbour as yourself, what greater act of love than to introduce someone to the Saviour who died to give them eternal life?

Whatever your occupation, the likelihood is that you come into contact with many people on a daily basis who may never set foot in a church. Their interaction with you might be the only time they ever experience the love of Jesus Christ. Whether you like the idea or not, you are a pastor, a missionary, and an evangelist at your place of work! So, if you thought the concept of walking in agape love in your workplace was a misnomer, think again!

In Matthew 5 v 13 - 16, Jesus was speaking to all believers when He said:

You are the salt of the earth; but if the salt loses its flavor, how shall it be seasoned? It is then good for nothing but to be thrown out and trampled underfoot by men. You are the light of the world. A city that is set on a hill cannot be hidden. Nor do they light a lamp and put it under a basket, but on a lampstand, and it gives light to all who are in the house. Let your light so shine before men, that they may see your good works and glorify your Father in heaven.

Jesus used the analogy of salt in this passage with good reason. Salt was used not only as a flavouring, but also as a means of preserving food. As His followers, we are supposed to be a moral preservative in a corrupt and decaying world. Our "flavour" should be influencing those around us and creating a thirst in them, as salt does, for the Living Water.

Jesus further explains this concept of the influence we are supposed to have by likening His children to a light that shines in the darkness. The world needs Christians to reflect the light of Jesus in order to illuminate the way to the Father. The purpose of light is to dispel darkness and reveal that which is unseen, in this case the truth of the Gospel. These principles of being salt and light in the workplace apply to all of us, regardless of whether we are the managing director, accountant, or cleaner. In the Kingdom of God, we are all called to share the Gospel and to love one another with God's kind of love.

Loving your *Boss* God's Way

One factor that is essential for making a job enjoyable and fulfilling is a positive and healthy relationship with your boss. Unfortunately, for many people, this can be a source of great stress and conflict. As believers in the workplace, we are called to walk in love and to submit to authority, but the fact is that some bosses are simply stressful to work for! Even bosses who claim to be believers can be demanding, unreasonable, obnoxious, and generally just not good leaders. In this situation, which I am sure is a reality for many of us, how do we manage our relationship with our bosses in a way that brings honour and glory to God?

In Ephesians 6 v 5 - 7 it says:

Bondservants, be obedient to those who are your masters according to the flesh, with fear and trembling, in sincerity of heart, as to Christ; not with eyeservice, as men-pleasers, but as bondservants of Christ, doing the will of God from the heart, with goodwill doing service, as to the Lord, and not to men, knowing that whatever good anyone does, he will receive the same from the Lord, whether he is a slave or free.

Paul is speaking in this Scripture about the relationship between slaves and their masters, but it does have application in the modern era in terms of the manager-employee relationship. Paul makes the point that although we may have people in authority over us in the natural, this is not the case in the spiritual realm. Jesus Christ is our only Master, and our obedience and service to Him must be our first priority. When we put Him first, other relationships will flourish in the overflow of our relationship with Him.

This Scripture also tells us that our hearts towards our bosses and our duties should be sincere. What does this actually mean? It means giving of your best at all times, not just when someone is watching! It also means having a willingness to give of yourself in order to ensure that the work you produce is of excellent quality. I am ashamed to admit that I, in the past, have been guilty of doing the minimum just to "get the job done". This is not giving of our best. Paul also reminds us that we should work as if we are working for the Lord, not for men. If Jesus asked you to do something would you not do it to the best of your ability and probably even go beyond what was asked of you? This principle is echoed in 1 Corinthians 10 v 31. It says:

Therefore, whether you eat or drink, or whatever you do, do all to the glory of God.

Once we realise that our job is not simply a means to earning a living, but rather an environment in which God has placed us to minister His love, then our focus starts to shift. We do not have to be in a position of authority or status in order to make a difference. We make a difference by doing what we do for the glory of God. The Lord did not call every one of us to be in ministry full-time, or to leave our homes and do mission work in foreign countries. Instead, He calls us all to work as if we were working for Him, regardless of how the world views our occupation. For example: if you are a painter, you need to be the best painter you can possibly be, knowing you are painting for Him. This attitude creates in us a spirit of excellence which will set us apart from others in the workplace and bring us favour and success.

In Daniel 6 v 3 - 4 it says:

Then this Daniel distinguished himself above the governors and satraps, because an excellent spirit was in him; and the king gave thought to setting him over the whole realm.

Daniel was favoured by the king because those around him recognized the Spirit of Excellence within him. Joseph was another example in the Scriptures of someone with an excellent spirit. He served all of his masters faithfully and consistently and was promoted because of it. Whether he was in the palace or the prison, he served as if he were serving the Lord.

Proverbs 22 v 29 confirms this biblical principle by saying:

Do you see a man who excels in his work? He will stand before kings; He will not stand before unknown men.

As a caution, it is important to recognise that excellence and perfectionism are not the same thing. Perfectionism is aimed at trying to please people, while excellence is focused on pleasing God. We are not called to be perfect, but we are called to be excellent!

Here are some suggestions to help you bring God's kind of love into your relationship with your boss.

1. Practice patience and kindness.
   Love suffers long and is kind – 1 Corinthians 13 v 4

   You will recall that these are the first two characteristics of agape love mentioned in 1 Corinthians 13. These principles should be the foundation of all of our relationships. It is especially difficult to react to an agitated, unreasonable, or critical boss with patience and kindness, but when we do so, the Holy Spirit is able to completely change the tone of the interaction.

2. Pray for your boss.
   But I say to you, love your enemies, bless those who curse you, do good to those who hate you, and pray for those who spitefully use you and persecute you – Matthew 5 v 44

Something miraculous happens when we pray for people with whom we experience conflict. Our hearts start to soften, and we begin to see them through God's eyes. Even if your boss is not a believer, Jesus counted him or her worthy of His death on the cross. That changes things, doesn't it? When we adopt this perspective, what we say and do comes from a place of God's infinite love and grace. Grace is defined as undeserved kindness. As Jesus showed us grace when He died for our sins, so we must extend grace to others – especially when we feel they don't deserve it!

3. Practice submission.

   Servants, be submissive to your masters with all fear, not only to the good and gentle, but also to the harsh. – 1 Peter 2 v 18

   Although many of us find this a difficult principle to put into practice, it is a biblical one! God has ordained many different spheres of authority in all aspects of life – government, marriage, family, church, and work - to name a few. How we respond to authority in our lives reflects the degree to which we have submitted to the Lordship of Jesus. That should cause every single one of us to pause for a moment and take stock! Submission does not mean that we have to be doormats. It simply means that we willingly rank ourselves under someone in authority over us. The keyword here is "willing". When we do this by choice, our attitude becomes one of serving, seeking the best for our boss, having a teachable spirit, and performing to the best of our ability.

Loving your *Colleagues* God's Way

I read a report a while ago of a JetBlue flight in America that was recently forced to make an emergency landing after one of the engines caught fire and caused the entire passenger cabin to fill with thick black smoke. Many of the passengers were afraid they were going to die. After leaving the plane, one passenger tweeted, "I'm so happy to be alive that I don't think I will ever be mean to anyone ever again!"

Isn't it amazing that all it takes is a perceived near-death experience to change our attitude towards others? As Christians, we have all been rescued from the wreckage of our lives. This alone should change the way we treat the people around us.

Our work colleagues are, in fact, the people with whom we spend the most time on a consistent basis. Those of us who work full-time are with our colleagues for up to 9 hours a day, 5 days a week. Compared to the frenetic morning rush and the weary evening hours we spend with our families, our colleagues actually get the "best" of us and our time. The workplace is an often colourful and crazy mixture of different ages, races, cultures, and religions. If you are lucky, you will find friends in your work environment who enrich your life and make your workdays much more pleasurable.

Inevitably though, there will be work colleagues who will get under your skin and annoy you! Greg Mohr, one of my lecturers at Charis Bible College, spoke about your "sandpaper person" – that person who always rubs you up the wrong way! I love this description! I have definitely come across a few sandpaper people in my time! It is in dealing with these types of people that we have the opportunity to expose them to God's kind of love. Anyone can love people that they like. It's how we deal with people who are difficult to get along with that shows the degree to which we are operating in love.

Practically, how do we show God's love to our colleagues?

1.   Pray

     Even though prayer is unseen, it is one of the most powerful things we can do for our colleagues. Take the time to listen to what your colleagues say in passing conversation so that you can identify areas where you can pray for them. This is especially important when it comes to those "sandpaper people"! We tend to avoid these people, but it is important that we make the effort to connect with them so that we can begin to understand their needs and daily struggles. You will find that it is not possible to pray for someone without feeling some measure of compassion towards them. This alone will begin to change how you relate to them.

2.   Be Intentional

     It is very tempting in the few minutes between meetings or at lunchtime to be occupied with checking emails or grabbing a cup of coffee, but this time is better invested in getting to know your co-workers and taking an interest in their lives outside the workplace. This will give you the opportunity to show concern and to make them feel valued. When you do this, trust begins to grow between you, which will then open a door for you to minister God's love to your colleagues.

3. Speak encouragement

    If I am sure of anything, it's that every single person on this earth needs encouragement! It is so easy to do and yet can have such a powerful effect. One word of encouragement can change the course of a person's whole day, and in some cases even their life! Find something positive to say to your colleagues, whether it is about their character, work, or appearance. Not only will it uplift them, but as you think of others before yourself, you will start to see all the good things about your co-workers that you never noticed before.

4. Seek opportunities to serve

    Ask God to show you the needs of those around you so that you can find opportunities to serve. Sometimes it may be something as small as making your colleague a cup of coffee, and other times it might mean taking a meal to their house. Once we begin to engage with our co-workers on a more personal level, we will start to recognize their challenges and difficulties more easily. By responding to their need, no matter how big or small, you can carry the light of Christ into their darkness.

Loving your *Employees* God's Way

Many people struggle with the idea that you can be an effective leader in the secular workplace while still remaining true to Christian values. For the born-again believer in a leadership position, there is no need to be authoritarian, critical or condescending when dealing with those who are subordinate to you. Jesus was a leader by nature and yet always dealt with people in a firm, kind, and compassionate manner.

By imitating Christ in the workplace, you will be able to effectively carry out your duties and responsibilities while also being a role model for those around you. As a Christian leader, you should firstly seek to bring honour and glory to God by demonstrating His kind of love, and secondly to inspire and influence those you are responsible for leading.

If we were to explore some of the characteristics of a Christian leader, we could say that a Christian leader:

1. Seeks God's Wisdom

    A Christian leader, no matter how important the position he holds, understands that he can accomplish nothing in his own strength apart from God. For this reason, a Christian leader will seek God's wisdom when making decisions and dealing with the people under his supervision.

If any of you lacks wisdom, let him ask of God, who gives to all liberally and without reproach, and it will be given to him.

James 1 v 5

2. Models Servant Leadership

    One of the qualities of agape love is that it is not self-seeking. A Christian leader places the best interests and welfare of his employees above his own and leads with humility. This encompasses taking the time to listen to employees, understand their challenges, and encourage them when need be.

    Let nothing be done through selfish ambition or conceit, but in lowliness of mind let each esteem others better than himself. Let each of you look out not only for his own interests, but also for the interests of others.

    Philippians 2 v 3 – 4

3. Acts with Integrity

    A Christian leader always promotes fairness, honesty and transparency when dealing with the people he works with. All decisions are made with integrity and in line with biblical moral standards.

    To do righteousness and justice is more acceptable to the Lord than sacrifice.

    Proverbs 21 v 3

4. Displays Love and Compassion

    As imitators of Christ, Christian leaders are called to show love and compassion to those who work under them. In the New Testament, we see Jesus performing miracles because He was moved by compassion for the person who was in need (Matthew 20 v 34). Compassion empowers Christian leaders to show genuine care and concern for their employees. This creates an environment of empathy and understanding in the workplace.

In conclusion, whatever your position or title, your ultimate goal is to glorify God in what you do. Whether you are making tea, making car parts or making million-dollar decisions, His wisdom and His presence should be tangible in your work. Coupled with this, you are called to be an imitator of Christ in how you interact with your superiors, colleagues, and subordinates.

Most people have become so used to only looking for God in the miraculous and the extraordinary that they forget to look for Him in the routine of everyday life. Finding Him in the seemingly mundane activities of your job will remind you of just how close He is at all times. He is with you in every meeting, as you sit at your desk, and as you go about your tasks. Being aware of His presence will literally transform your everyday life and the lives of those around you.

CHAPTER
Eight

Agape Love in the World

You can give without loving, but you cannot love without giving. – Amy Carmichael

AS WE COME TO THE FINAL CHAPTER OF THIS JOURNEY, WE are going to find out how we, as disciples of Jesus Christ, are called to love those who are strangers to us. This is such a vast topic that it could be a book on its own! Loving people that we don't know isn't something that comes naturally to the majority of us. In other words, it is not part of our human nature.

As Holy Spirit-filled Christians, however, it is part of our spiritual nature. The fruits of the Holy Spirit are listed in Galatians 5 as being "love, joy, peace, longsuffering, kindness, goodness, faithfulness, gentleness, self-control". How often have we failed to demonstrate these qualities when interacting with the painfully slow cashier at the grocery store, or the beggar knocking on the car window at the traffic light?

In Hebrews 13 v 2, it is written:

Do not forget to entertain strangers, for by so doing some have unwittingly entertained angels.

Where the New King James Version talks about "entertaining" strangers, other Bible translations speak of showing "hospitality" to those who approach us. Hospitality is defined as "the friendly and generous reception and entertainment of guests, visitors, or strangers". This Scripture tells us a few important things.

Firstly, we need to be mindful of the people whom the Lord brings across our path. The person that you dismiss so easily may have a divine appointment with you! I think we often miss out on what the Lord wants to do through us, and sometimes to us, because we are too quick to overlook people that we come into contact with in the ordinary activities of life. Secondly, by pointing out that we may be entertaining angels, the writer of this Scripture is highlighting that all people have value and are worthy of our time, resources, and effort. We may not know them, but we are to consider them worthy of our hospitality, regardless of their appearance or our perception of them. We need to see every person as an opportunity for us to operate in the agape love of God!

Jesus Himself addressed the principle of showing hospitality to strangers in Matthew 25 v 35 - 40 when He said:

For I was hungry and you gave Me food; I was thirsty and you gave Me drink; I was a stranger and you took Me in; I was naked and you clothed Me; I was sick and you visited Me; I was in prison and you came to Me. Then the righteous will answer Him, saying, 'Lord, when did we see You hungry and feed You, or thirsty and give You drink? When did we see You a stranger and take You in, or naked and clothe You? Or when did we see You sick, or in prison, and come to You?' And the King will answer and say to them, 'Assuredly, I say to you, inasmuch as you did it to one of the least of these My brethren, you did it to Me.

When we show hospitality to strangers and love them with God's kind of love, it is the same as if we were doing it to Jesus. Now that is food for thought, isn't it? I bet we would all react very differently if we answered the knock at the front door to find Jesus standing there rather than yet another hungry beggar.

Living in a third world country like South Africa, where there is so much poverty and desperate need, I often find myself overwhelmed by the magnitude of the problem. It is almost as if the sheer volume of people in need paralyses me and prevents me from reaching out at all. It feels seemingly impossible, as one person, to make the slightest bit of difference because the need is so great. Have you ever felt like that? I am often reminded of the illustration of the little girl saving starfish on the beach. In case you don't know it, this is how it goes.

The Starfish Saviour

A young girl was walking along a beach that was strewn with thousands of starfish that had been washed up during a terrible storm. As she came to each starfish, she would stop, pick it up, and throw it back into the ocean.

A man stood and watched her with amusement.

She had been doing this for some time when he approached her and said, "Little girl, what are you doing? It's not going to make any difference, there are too many!".

The girl paused and thought for a moment. Then she bent down, picked up another starfish, and hurled it as far as she could into the ocean. She looked up at the man and replied, "Well, it made a difference for that one!".

This illustration is so applicable to the situation we face in South Africa. Yes, the need is massive and overwhelming, but we still need to make a difference where we can. Even if you only reach out to one person, you have made an impact in someone's life.

There is a tendency among Christians to think that the "neighbours" we have been commanded to love are those who live around us and those we come into contact with on a regular basis. This is simply not true. I think we sometimes use this rationale as an excuse not to love the ones we perceive to be unlovely. If we ever have any doubts about who our "neighbour" is, we only have to read the parable of the Good Samaritan to find the answer. We find this Scripture in Luke 10 v 25 – 37.

And behold, a certain lawyer stood up and tested Him, saying, "Teacher, what shall I do to inherit eternal life?"

He said to him, "What is written in the law? What is your reading of it?"

So he answered and said, " 'You shall love the Lord your God with all your heart, with all your soul, with all your strength, and with all your mind,' and 'your neighbor as yourself.' "

And He said to him, "You have answered rightly; do this and you will live."

But he, wanting to justify himself, said to Jesus, "And who is my neighbor?"

Then Jesus answered and said: "A certain man went down from Jerusalem to Jericho, and fell among thieves, who stripped him of his clothing, wounded him, and departed, leaving him half dead. Now by chance a certain priest came down that road. And when he saw him, he passed by on the other side. Likewise a Levite, when he arrived at the place, came and looked, and passed by on the other side. But a certain Samaritan, as he journeyed, came where he was. And when he saw him, he had compassion. So he went to him and bandaged his wounds, pouring on oil and wine; and he set him on his own animal, brought him to an inn, and took care of him. On the next day, when he departed, he took out two denarii, gave them to the innkeeper, and said to him, 'Take care of him; and whatever more you spend, when I come again, I will repay you.' So which of these three do you think was neighbor to him who fell among the thieves?"

And he said, "He who showed mercy on him."

Then Jesus said to him, "Go and do likewise."

The lawyer who was questioning Jesus in this Scripture was seeking to justify himself and his actions. We can see that he knew the Old Testament law very well, as he quoted the exact same Scriptures in Deuteronomy and Leviticus that Jesus quoted when He was asked in Matthew 22 about which commandment was the greatest. This lawyer knew that he had not loved everyone as he loved himself and was searching for an interpretation of the Scripture that would justify his actions. He, like many of us, was hoping to define his neighbour as those close to him, those he knew he had treated with love. Jesus used this parable to illustrate that a "neighbour" is any human being who crosses our path who needs help.

As an aside, it is important to acknowledge that we cannot meet the needs of every person in the world. This is not what Jesus was trying to teach. The man in the parable who was attacked was directly in the path of the priest, the Levite, and the Samaritan. Each of them had to make a choice either to stop and help, or to walk around him. We need to be mindful of the people the Lord places in our path and use the opportunities that are presented to us. This helps put into perspective the problem of who to help when the need is so great. We cannot help everyone, but we can help those brought to us by the Lord. We can choose not to walk around them.

Jesus also specifically used the example of a Samaritan in this parable to make a point. There was a lot of racial and religious strife between the Samaritan people and the Jews. The priest and the Levite were countrymen of the wounded man, yet they did not help him. The one who stopped to help was the man's "enemy" by birth, yet he was the true "neighbour". In a country like South Africa where so much racial, political, and cultural tension still exists, this story reminds us that all people are our neighbours, regardless of geography or genetics.

1 Samuel 16 v 7 tells us:

But the Lord said to Samuel, "Do not look at his appearance or at his physical stature, because I have refused him. For the Lord does not see as man sees; for man looks at the outward appearance, but the Lord looks at the heart.

If God looks at the heart of man and not the outward appearance, then we should strive to do the same. When we operate in God's kind of love towards people, we need to see them through God's eyes.

Let's look at a few examples of how Jesus showed love to strangers during His earthly ministry.

1.   Jesus showed kindness to the marginalized.

In Luke 19 v 1 – 6, we read the account of Jesus and Zacchaeus.

Then Jesus entered and passed through Jericho. Now behold, there was a man Zacchaeus who was a chief tax collector, and he was rich. And he sought to see who Jesus was, but could not because of the crowd, for he was of short stature. So he ran ahead and climbed up into a sycamore tree to see Him, for He was going to pass that way. And when Jesus came to the place, He looked up and saw him, and said to him, "Zacchaeus, make haste and come down, for today I must stay at your house." So he made haste and came down, and received Him joyfully. But when they saw it, they all complained, saying, "He has gone to be a guest with a man who is a sinner.

Jesus singles Zacchaeus out from a crowd of people and chooses to spend the day with him. Zacchaeus was disliked and made fun of by the people, firstly because he was a tax collector and secondly, because of his diminutive stature. Jesus knew how His love, time and kindness would change Zacchaeus's life.

In the same way, Jesus did not shy away from the many lepers who approached him for healing during His ministry. In Matthew 8 v 1 – 4, we read an account of Jesus laying hands on a leper in order to heal him. Lepers were so feared and reviled that they were forced to live outside the walls of the cities and were required to ring a bell as they walked so that people could avoid them. Imagine the impact it had on them when Jesus not only came close to them, but actually touched them!

2. Jesus healed the sick.
    There are so many accounts of Jesus healing the sick during His ministry that they are too numerous to mention. There is no doubt that healing was always His will, and thus the will of Father God. Jesus never turned anyone away who came to Him seeking healing. One account in particular has always stood out for me because it shows Jesus' heart behind His actions.

    We read in Matthew 20 v 29 - 34:
    Now as they went out of Jericho, a great multitude followed Him. And behold, two blind men sitting by the road, when they

heard that Jesus was passing by, cried out, saying, "Have mercy on us, O Lord, Son of David!"

Then the multitude warned them that they should be quiet; but they cried out all the more, saying, "Have mercy on us, O Lord, Son of David!"

So Jesus stood still and called them, and said, "What do you want Me to do for you?"

They said to Him, "Lord, that our eyes may be opened." So Jesus had compassion and touched their eyes. And immediately their eyes received sight, and they followed Him.

What strikes me about this Scripture is that Jesus was moved by compassion for the blind men. We also see His compassion for people mentioned in Mark 1 v 41 and Matthew 14 v 14. Godly compassion is an essential element if we are to imitate Christ and operate in agape love towards people, especially when praying for healing. If we are indifferent to people's physical suffering, we will not see healing miracles take place. Compassion releases God's healing power to work through us.

3. Jesus fed the hungry.

In Matthew 14 v 15 – 21 we read:

When it was evening, His disciples came to Him, saying, "This is a deserted place, and the hour is already late. Send the multitudes away, that they may go into the villages and buy themselves food."

But Jesus said to them, "They do not need to go away. You give them something to eat."

And they said to Him, "We have here only five loaves and two fish."

He said, "Bring them here to Me." Then He commanded the multitudes to sit down on the grass. And He took the five loaves and the two fish, and looking up to heaven, He blessed and broke and gave the loaves to the disciples; and the disciples gave to the multitudes. So they all ate and were filled, and they took up twelve baskets full of the fragments that remained. Now those who had eaten were about five thousand men, besides women and children."

Jesus was not only concerned with the spiritual needs of people. In order for people to experience God's kind of love, we also sometimes need to address their physical needs. All through this journey, we have been reminded that God's kind of love is action, not just words. We need to act where possible to alleviate physical suffering.

4.   Jesus preached the Good News.

In Isaiah 6, we find a prophecy about the ministry of Jesus which was written more than 700 years before His birth. In Luke 4 v 17 – 21, Jesus is preaching in the synagogue in Nazareth and He confirms that He is indeed the Messiah about whom Isaiah prophesied.

He was handed the book of the prophet Isaiah. And when He had opened the book, He found the place where it was written:

"The Spirit of the Lord is upon Me,
Because He has anointed Me
To preach the gospel to the poor;
He has sent Me to heal the brokenhearted,
To proclaim liberty to the captives
And recovery of sight to the blind,
To set at liberty those who are oppressed;
To proclaim the acceptable year of the Lord."

Then He closed the book, and gave it back to the attendant and sat down. And the eyes of all who were in the synagogue were fixed on Him. And He began to say to them, "Today this Scripture is fulfilled in your hearing."

Jesus was anointed by God to preach the gospel. Everywhere He went, He shared the good news that through Him the forgiveness of sins and the free gift of eternal life is available to all who believe.

The Bible tells us in John 17 v 3:
And this is eternal life, that they may know You, the only true God, and Jesus Christ whom You have sent.

What better way to love people than to offer them relationship with Him and a place in His kingdom?

5.   Jesus prayed and interceded.

In John 17, just before His betrayal and arrest in the Garden of Gethsemane, we read an account of how Jesus prayed, firstly for Himself and then for His disciples. In verse 20, Jesus prays for all future believers. He knew that after His death, and in the centuries to come, believers would face many difficulties. But because He knew the power of prayer, He went to His Father and interceded for us as follows:

I do not pray for these alone, but also for those who will believe in Me through their word; that they all may be one, as You, Father, are in Me, and I in You; that they also may be one in Us, that the world may believe that You sent Me. And the glory which You gave Me I have given them, that they may be one just as We are one: I in them, and You in Me; that they may be made perfect in one, and that the world may know that You have sent Me, and have loved them as You have loved Me.

How amazing that the Son of God would pray for us, especially in His last hours on earth! Even more, because His love for us never ends, He is still interceding for us from His seat at the right hand of Father God!

Now that we have seen some examples of how Jesus showed agape love to people He came into contact with, how do we go about doing the same?

Ephesians 5 v 1 – 2 tells us very clearly that we are to be imitators of Christ.

Therefore be imitators of God as dear children. And walk in love, as Christ also has loved us and given Himself for us, an offering and a sacrifice to God for a sweet-smelling aroma.

And yes, it really is that simple! If you want to show God's kind of love to the people in need who cross your path, just imitate Jesus!

In other words:

1. Show kindness to the marginalized and the outcast.
2. Pray for and heal the sick.
3. Feed the hungry.
4. Share the Good News of the Gospel.
5. Intercede and pray for those in difficult circumstances.

A Note on *Godly* Giving

In countries like South Africa, where there is so much poverty, unemployment, and hunger, the easiest and most obvious way to show love to strangers is through giving. This might be in the form of food, clothing, or finances. A lot is preached in churches about giving, and many

Christians end up feeling guilty that they are not financially able to help every person they come across. On any given day, for example, I might drive past 10 to 15 people begging at the traffic lights. If I were to give to every one of those people on a daily basis, I would seriously jeopardise my family's financial well-being. During my time in ministry, I came across people who would give so much and so freely that they would not have enough left to feed themselves or meet their financial obligations. This is not the way that God wants us to use the resources that He has given us. It is important that we realise that there is a vast difference between indiscriminate giving and Godly giving.

We should always be mindful of the motivation behind our giving. The heart behind our giving is more important to God than the gift. The Bible does say in Mark 10 v 30 that when we give for His sake, we will receive one hundredfold back in this life. This does not mean, however, that we should give with the express purpose of getting something back. I have met many people who give because they think it will "force" God to meet some need that they have. This is the wrong motivation and will never cause us to prosper.

In the beginning of this journey, we read in 1 Corinthians 13 v 3:

And though I bestow all my goods to feed the poor, and though I give my body to be burned, but have not love, it profits me nothing.

The motivation for our giving has to be love. This means that our giving must be directed by Love Himself.

The Bible also tells us in 2 Corinthians 9 v 7:

So let each one give as he purposes in his heart, not grudgingly or of necessity; for God loves a cheerful giver.

The Lord wants us to give when we have the desire to do so, not out of guilt or obligation. If you give because you feel pressured, then it is not the right time to give. Giving is only right when we are led to do so by the Holy Spirit and the desire in our heart is to show God's kind of love to those in need.

The quote by Amy Carmichael that was used at the beginning of this chapter perfectly sums up the relationship between love and giving and it is a fitting conclusion to this subject.

"You can give without loving, but you cannot love without giving."

Conclusion

Let's recap for a moment and read the Scripture in Matthew 22 v 37 – 39 that started us on this journey.

Jesus said to him, "'You shall love the Lord your God with all your heart, with all your soul, and with all your mind.' This is the first and great commandment. And the second is like it: 'You shall love your neighbour as yourself.'

I am sure that many of you started this book feeling like Jesus was commanding you to do something impossible! My prayer is that you have come to realise that loving your neighbour is entirely possible with Him by your side! It is not something that will happen overnight, but as you continue to seek Him with all your heart, soul, and mind, you will day by day be conformed to His image. This is not meant to be a heavy or onerous task that we have to strive to achieve; it is meant to be an overflow of what He has placed on the inside of us. Christ in us already loves our neighbours! All we have to do is be mindful, intentional, and available, and allow His love to flow through us to impact the world.

What it means to be Born Again

Christianity differs from all the other religions in a very specific way. It is the only religion whose followers believe in and acknowledge that we need a Saviour. All other religions believe there is a God (or many gods), but that salvation can be earned through self-denial, holy living, and charitable works. True Christianity does not place any responsibility on the individual, except to believe in Jesus. We are all sinners (Romans 3 v 23), and the only way we can be set free from the consequences of sin, which is death, is to receive the free gift of salvation offered by Jesus through His sacrifice on the cross.

Jesus said in John 14 v 6:

I am the way, the truth, and the life. No one comes to the Father except through Me.

Many other religions acknowledge the existence of Jesus, but they do not accept Him as the Son of God. They all recognise that He was a good man and a prophet, but nothing more. The Scripture quoted above leaves no room for doubt. No one can receive salvation unless they recognize that Jesus is their Saviour, and the only way to the Father.

When sin came into the world through Adam and Eve, it caused a divide between God and man. Under the Old Testament Law, people made animal sacrifices to atone for their sins. This was something that had to be done repeatedly, as every sin required payment through the shedding of blood. God loved you and me so much that He sent Jesus to be the atonement for the sins of all mankind, once, for all time. His blood that was shed on the cross paid for your sins and mine – past, present and future. Because of His sacrifice, God remembers your sin no more and you are holy and righteous in His sight. The sin that once stood as a barrier between you and God, has been removed forever! What an amazing Saviour we have! All we have to do is believe and receive!

The Bible says in Romans 10 v 9 – 10:

That if you confess with your mouth the Lord Jesus and believe in your heart that God has raised Him from the dead, you will be saved. For with the heart one believes unto righteousness, and with the mouth confession is made unto salvation.

It is that simple! If you believe in your heart that Jesus died for you, and you confess it out loud, you will be saved!

If you have never accepted Jesus as your Lord and Saviour, you can do so right now! It is the best decision you will ever make! The moment you do this, your spirit is washed clean and becomes brand new! You have been born again!

Pray this prayer out loud:

"Jesus, I confess that I am a sinner and that I need a Saviour. I believe in my heart that you died to pay for my sins, and that God raised you from the dead. Please come and be Lord of my life. By faith in Your Word, I accept Your gift of salvation. Thank you for saving me!"

If you prayed this prayer, I would encourage you to contact a friend, family member or local church who can help you to understand more fully what it means to have taken this important step! This new life is meant to be lived in fellowship with other believers who can encourage you and help you to grow in your relationship with the Lord.

Baptism in the Holy Spirit

As a born-again child of God, you have access to the supernatural power of the Holy Spirit! Jesus Himself did not begin His earthly ministry until the Holy Spirit came upon Him at the moment of His baptism in water. If the Son of God needed to be empowered by the Holy Spirit, how much more do we need it?

After Jesus' death and resurrection, He told His disciples in Acts 1 v 4 to wait in Jerusalem for the "Promise of the Father" which was the Holy Spirit. He said in verse 5:

For John truly baptized with water, but you shall be baptized with the Holy Spirit not many days from now.

Even though the disciples had the greatest news of Jesus' resurrection to report to the world, the Lord told them to wait until they received the Holy Spirit. This leaves no doubt that baptism in the Holy Spirit is something we all need in order to be fully equipped to live this new life.

In the same way in which you received salvation, you only have to ask for the gift of the Holy Spirit. In Luke 11 v 13 it says:

If you then, being evil, know how to give good gifts to your children, how much more will your heavenly Father give the Holy Spirit to those who ask Him!

All you have to do is ask, believe, and receive!

One of the signs that you have been filled with the Holy Spirit is speaking in tongues. Tongues is a heavenly prayer language that is available to every believer. It is a language that you will not understand with your natural mind, but it is your born-again spirit communicating directly with God. Once you have received the Holy Spirit, syllables and words you don't recognise will rise up from your heart. All you have to do is speak them out loud by faith! When you speak in tongues, you release God's power and you build yourself up in your spirit. (1 Corinthians 14 v 4). This is not something that you have no control over – you decide when you want to speak in tongues and when to stop. The Holy Spirit is always gentle with us!

If you want to receive the Holy Spirit, all you have to do is ask as follows:

"Lord, I recognize that I need Your supernatural power in order to live this new life. Please come and fill me with Your Holy Spirit. By faith I receive it right now. Thank you for baptizing me and thank you for the gift of tongues. Holy Spirit, you are welcome in my life!"

Some people have a tangible experience during baptism and others don't feel anything at all. If you believed in your heart when you prayed, then God's Word promises that you received!

Please reach out to someone who can help you on this journey to understanding what just happened in your life and how to walk in this awesome power that you now have access to! You are no longer simply human – part of you is wall-to-wall Holy Spirit!